SLIM Chance **FAT** Hope
Society's Obsession with Thinness

Catherine Tay

'I would really like to commend Catherine Tay and her superbly assembled team of relevant experts and significant lay persons for putting in such a very formidable effort to bring to print this excellent and comprehensive book. It helps modern day parents and their teenagers deal with the various aspects of the slimming matter. It would be slim chance & fat hope that this paperback book would not make it onto the must-read booklist of especially parents with teenager kids in Singapore and beyond. I strongly recommend that this book be added onto the shelves of our national and schools' libraries as well as to personal collection too.'

Assoc. Prof. (Dr.) Yeo Jin Fei

Chief
Senior Consultant
Department of Oral and Maxillofacial Surgery
National University Hospital, Singapore

'This is an excellent book that is timely.

It dispels many myths about weight management and gives sound advice and guidelines on body-image healthcare.

It is highly readable, pleasant, interesting and amusing at times and definitely informative and instructive, highly recommended.'

Clinical Professor (Dr.) Low Cheng Hock

Justice of Peace
President, NHG College
Associate Dean, Tan Tock Seng Hospital
Senior Consultant, Department of General Surgery,
Tan Tock Seng Hospital, Singapore

SLIM Chance   FAT Hope

'There are always hesitation and doubts before a slimming programme but the book will advise us on the correct and healthy ways to achieve it.'

Mr. Huang Wenyong
MediaCorp (TV) Artiste

'This is another commendable effort by Assoc. Prof. Catherine Tay. Just fresh from the publication of her book on *Infectious Diseases Laws and SARS*, she has now turned the Slim 10 episode into another opportunity for public education by bringing together various professionals to write on issues pertinent to the case. Informative and readable, the book should appeal especially to those seeking to know more about obesity, slimming and consumer protection and rights.'

Dr. Ang Ah Ling
Senior Consultant Psychiatrist
Institute of Mental Health / Woodbridge Hospital
Singapore

'The relentless pursuit of thinness by certain members of the population is a very 21st century phenomenon. *Slim Chance Fat Hope* discusses the medical-psychological-sociological-legal aspects in a readable and down-to-earth manner.'

Clinical Assoc. Prof. (Dr.) Wong Kim Eng
Chairman Medical Board
Institute of Mental Health / Woodbridge Hospital, Singapore

'Assoc. Prof. Tay and her team of authors should be commended for producing this excellent book *Slim Chance Fat Hope*. This comprehensive book on obesity, presents the Dos and Don'ts to slimming. The book delves into the definition of obesity and the human perception and obsession of attaining a slim figure which equates to beauty. It has resulted in people indulging in slimming. The health hazards of slimming through the injudicious use of slimming pill were well illustrated by the recent Slim 10 saga. The book provides the readers with insights into the medical perspective (including the genetic basis of obesity), consumer rights, the legal perspective in the Slim 10 case the community response and responsibility in healthy lifestyle. Each chapter is written by experts in their own field.

This book is a must to those who wish to enter into the journey of body slimming to get an insight of what is in store for them.'

Clinical Professor (Dr.) Goh Chee Leok
Medical Director
National Skin Centre, Singapore

'Obesity is becoming increasingly recognised as a public health issue with medical, socioeconomic and cultural implications. This book has succeeded in portraying obesity in its different dimensions and from various perspectives. It completely debunks the myth that obesity is merely cosmetic.'

Dr Wee Wei Keong
Director
Health for Life Programme
Alexandra Hospital, Singapore

SLIM Chance FAT Hope

'**I** do not envy the woman of today – having to juggle the multiple roles of wife, companion, mother, wage-earner, cook, cleaner, and in addition having the responsibility to keep the flames of marital bliss alive by maintaining her pre-nuptial figure. No wonder so many women have succumbed to the various slimming ads and fads.

Triggered by the Slim 10 incident, this book comprehensively examines the issues related to anorexia, obesity and slimming. Although it is a multi-authored book, the topics are strung together in a cohesive manner and flow naturally with an easy-to-read writing style.

My congratulations to the editor, Catherine Tay, and the publisher for coming out with this timely and very interesting publication.'

Prof. (Dr.) Lee Eng Hin
Director, Division of Graduate Medical Studies
Faculty of Medicine and Former Dean of Medical Faculty
National University of Singapore

'**T** here is no perfect body. God gave us different shapes, sizes and weights. The fat and also thin people will always be spending money to strive to remain slim, their whole life.
This is well illustrated in this book.'

Assoc. Prof. (Dr.) Giam Yoke Chin
Senior Consultant Dermatologist
National Skin Centre, Singapore

'*Slim Chance Fat Hope* provides an in-depth look into the current issues of obesity, slimming, and the social attitudes towards these topics in Singapore. The varied inputs by members of the medical, legal, and social science fraternities, provide both factual, as well as personal insights, which make for an interesting read. '

Dr. Tan Huay Cheem

Senior Consultant Cardiologist
Clinical Director, Coronary Intervention
Chief, Cardiac Department, National University Hospital
Singapore

'A must read book for all who are considering a weight management plan! '

Dr. Alphonsus Tay

Partner- Apollonia Dental Surgery
Singapore

'*Slim Chance Fat Hope* aptly describes a weighty problem that has tormented many youths and young adults from all walks of life. Catherine Tay has been able to collate in this very readable book, opinions of different professionals. This is a simple yet comprehensive and holistic book on the subject. Well done. '

Dr. Lionel Lim

Senior Consultant Psychiatrist
L P Clinic Pte Ltd
Mount Elizabeth Medical Centre, Singapore

'Obesity is not a cosmetic problem. It is not even a medical problem. It is a human problem for it encompasses political, cultural, economic, legal, social and behavioural dimensions. Therefore this multi-authored book entitled *Slim Chance Fat Hope* edited by Assoc. Prof. Catherine Tay is not only timely but is just "what the doctor ordered".

Driven by the Slim 10 tragedy which need not have happened at all if our people are more health-literate, it is the only book I know on obesity that addresses all these topics in a clear and readable style in a single volume.

I enjoy in particular reading the interviews with Moses Lim and Hossan Leong, two actors with very different proportions but both accepting what they are. It is not necessary to look like any of the glamour queens in Caldecott Hill or Hollywood to be healthy. If you are obese lose up to 10–15% of your present weight over 6–12 months and you will reduce the risk of heart attacks, strokes, diabetes and knee arthritis by one-third. Everyone can do this with the help of a dietician and a supportive family.

Learn what to eat and what to avoid and how to cook. Never feel miserable while you are on a diet or else it is not going to work long term. Always accompany a weight loss programme with some form of moderate exercise.

Such common-sense pearls of wisdom are found scattered in the book. Read it for it may save your life.'

Emeritus Prof. Feng Pao Hsii
Emeritus Consultant Physician/Rheumatologist
Adjunct Professor of Medicine, Medical Faculty
National University of Singapore

Contents

SLIM Chance FAT Hope

Editor's
Preface

Catherine Tay Swee Kian

Master of Laws (London)
Bachelor of Laws (Hons) (London)
Barrister-at-Law (United Kingdom)
Advocate & Solicitor (Singapore)

Associate Professor
Department of Business Policy
NUS Business School
National University of Singapore

T he recent High Court decision of *Andrea Heidi De Cruz v Guangzhou Yuzhitang Health Products Co Ltd & Ors* (2003) — (the "Slim 10 case") — is a landmark case for product liability in Singapore. Apart from the Consumer Protection (Fair Trading) Act, the Slim 10 case is also an important development for consumer protection. The Slim 10 case is the launch pad for this book as the book title *Slim Chance Fat Hope* aptly describes the global obsession of persons trying to stay slim!

Do enjoy this book for the different perspectives and viewpoints about the science of obesity, slimming, dieting, body image, consumer rights and product safety written by various authors — medical doctors, scientists, psychiatrists, dieticians, lawyers, lecturers, media journalists, social commentators — who are experienced in their own fields. This book thus provides for serious discussion as well as for educating the mind.

For so kindly writing the blurbs to this book, I would like to thank Prof. Christopher Tang, Prof. (Dr.) Feng Pao Hsii, Assoc. Prof. (Dr.) Yeo Jin Fei, Mr. Huang Wenyong, Prof. (Dr.) Lee Eng Hin, Clin. Prof. (Dr.) Goh Chee Leok, Clin. Prof. Low Cheng Hock, Clin. Assoc. Prof. (Dr.) Wong Kim Eng, Dr. Ang Ah Ling, Assoc. Prof. (Dr.) Giam Yoke Chin, Dr. Tan Huay Cheem, Dr. Wee Wei Keong, Dr. Alphonsus Tay and Dr. Lionel Lim.

March 2004

About the Editor

atherine Tay Swee Kian is an Associate Professor lecturing law at the National University of Singapore (NUS), Department of Business Policy, NUS Business School. She also lectures medical law and biomedical ethics in the Faculty of Dentistry, NUS. She also supervises medical students in legal aspects of medical practice in the Special Study Module at the Faculty of Medicine, NUS. She is an Advocate and Solicitor of the Supreme Court of Singapore and a barrister-at-law (of Lincoln's Inn, United Kingdom). She is an author of 26 law books.

Prof. Tay is a member of the Research and Ethics Committee of Alexandra Hospital. She is a member of the Institutional Review Board of SingHealth Polyclinics. She is also a member of the National Healthcare Group (NHG) Domain Specific Review Board which is tasked to review the scientific and ethical aspects of research protocols. Prof. Tay was a medical legal adviser of the Institute of Mental Health/Woodbridge Hospital.

Prof. Tay studied law at Queen Mary College, University of London and graduated with a Bachelor of Laws with Honours in 1977 and with a Master of Laws in 1979, in which she specialised in Company, Shipping, Insurance and Marine Insurance Laws. She was called to the English Bar by Lincoln's Inn in 1978. She did her pupillage under the Honourable Lady Mary Hogg in London and returned to Singapore in the law firm of Rodyk & Davidson. She won the Aw Boon Haw and Aw Boon Par Memorial Prize for the overall best student in 1980 during her postgraduate practical law course in Singapore. She was called to the Singapore Bar in 1980.

In February 1984 and July 1986, Prof. Tay made representations to the Parliamentary Select Committee on the Companies (Amendment) Bills 1984 and 1986. She is a member of the Board of Advisors of the Arena Country Club.

Prof. Tay has published the following law books:

- *Company Formation Practice Manual* (1983, Malayan Law Journal)
- *Bankruptcy — The Law & Practice* (1984, Butterworths)

- *Judicial Management* (1987, Malayan Law Journal)
- *A Law Handbook for Businessmen* (1990, Print & Publish)
- *Directors' Duties & Liabilities including Insider Trading* (1985, Times Books International)
- *Your Rights as a Consumer — A Guide to Sale of Goods, Hire-Purchase and Small Claims Tribunal* (1986, Times Books International)
- *Contract Law including E-Commerce Law* (1987, Times Books International)
- *Hotel and Catering Law* (1992, SNP Publishers Pte Ltd)
- *Investing in Stocks and Shares* (1993, Specialist Press)
- *How to Write a Will?* (2003, Big Publications Pte Ltd)
- *How to Collect Your Debts? - A Guide to Bankruptcy Law* (1994, SNP Publishers Pte Ltd)
- *Buying and Selling Your Property - An Essential Guide to the Singapore Property Market* (1994, Times Books International)
- *Investing in HDB Property* (1995, Times Books International)
- *Investing in Real Estate* (1996, Longman Singapore Publishers Pte Ltd)
- *Copyright and The Protection of Designs* (1997, SNP Publishers Pte Ltd)
- *A Guide to Protecting Your Ideas, Inventions, Trade Marks & Products* (1997, Times Books International)
- *Resolving Disputes by Arbitration* (1998, Singapore University Press)
- *E-Commerce Law* (2000, Times Books International)
- *Medical Negligence* (2001, Times Books International)

- *Know Your Rights — Employment Law* (2002, Times Books International)
- *Infectious Diseases Law & SARS* (2003, Times Books International).

Prof. Tay has contributed and published legal articles in established international refereed journals, such as *BIOETHICS*, the *Hong Kong Journal of Emergency Medicine*, the (United Kingdom) *Journal of Business Law*, the (United Kingdom) *Company Lawyer* and the (United Kingdom) *Insolvency Law & Practice*, (United Kingdom) *Tolley's Professional Negligence* and the *Singapore Dental Journal*. She also contributes to high-quality legal publications of local importance and relevance such as *The Malayan Law Journal*, the *Securities Industry Review*, the *Singapore Management Review* and *The Singapore Law Gazette*, an official publication of The Law Society of Singapore as well as *The New Gazette* (the official publication of The Law Society of Hong Kong).

Prof. Tay was a committee member of the editorial board of the *Singapore Accountant Journal, Journal of the Institute of Certified Public Accountants of Singapore* and the (United Kingdom) *Company Lawyer*. She was on the Board of Overseas Editors for the (United Kingdom) *Journal of Financial Crime*, an official publication of the Cambridge International Symposium on Economic Crime. She was a member of the editorial board of the *Singapore Polytechnic Graduate Guild Journal*. She has presented papers at many conferences and seminars on Business Law, Biomedical Ethics and Medical law,

Company and Insolvency Laws both overseas and in Singapore. She is an examiner on law subjects for a number of professional bodies in Singapore and overseas. She conducts in-house seminars for hospitals, banks, statutory boards, hotels, commercial firms and companies, clubs and associations.

Prof. Tay lectures on medical law and biomedical ethics in hospitals such as Singapore General Hospital, National Heart Centre, National Skin Centre, National Healthcare Group College, Changi General Hospital, Toa Payoh Hospital, SingHealth Polyclinics at Tampines and Bedok, Alexandra Hospital, National University Hospital, Mount Elizabeth Hospital including the Department of Anatomy, Faculty of Medicine, National University of Singapore and the National Healthcare Group College. She has lectured in seminars and workshops in medical ethics and law in February 2000 organised by the Singapore Dental Association (SDA) Ethics Committee where the number of CDE points accredited was 4. In March 2003, she was an invited speaker at the "Third ASEAN Conference in Primary Health Care" organised by the Perak Medical Practitioners Society in Ipoh, Malaysia.

Prof. Tay is a legal consultant appearing on many television segments produced by the Television Corporation of Singapore. She speaks on legal subjects on MediaCorp radio weekly. She has co-hosted a weekly talk show "In the Eyes of the Law" on NTUC RadioHeart. She was a consultant to a MediaCorp television series on consumer laws "What's Your Case" on Channel 5.

Prof. Tay participates actively in several professional and charitable organisations for which she has received several titles and awards, including the Miss Singapore-International Charity

Queen in 1990 and 1991 and Miss Singapore-World University Charity Queen in 1992. She was a committee member of the Advice and Referral Service in the Singapore Council of Women's Organisation. From 1990 to 2000, she was the President of the Business and Professional Women's Association, Singapore. In March 1992, she was a nominee for the Women of the Year Award. In May 1994, she received the Paul Harris Fellow Award from Rotary International in recognition of her community service.

Medical/Science
Perspective

The Management of Body Weight

Dr. Tey Beng Hea
Senior Consultant Endocrinologist
Department of Medicine
Director
Weight Management Programme
Alexandra Hospital

T he Slim 10 incident which first surfaced in early 2002 and the subsequent avalanche of media reports concerning the use of OTC (Over-The-Counter) slimming products have pointed to the widespread use of OTC slimming products in Singapore particularly among our young female population, many of whom are not overweight or obese. A recent survey on Singaporeans' perception of obesity by A C Nielsen, (a reputable international market research organisation) and initiated by Roche Singapore Pte. Ltd., has shown that although one in three Singaporeans consider themselves overweight, one in two of those considered overweight are willing to take slimming medications to help them reduce weight. These observations showed that misconceptions of obesity and weight management are prevalent in our population and would need to be addressed.

Definition of obesity

The World Health Organisation (WHO) defined obesity as a condition of excessive fat accumulation in the body to the extent that health and well-being are adversely affected.

The use of Body Mass Index (BMI) (derived from weight divided by height squared, measured in kg/m^2) to compare the physique of man was first advocated in the 19th century. The WHO classified weight categories in adults using BMI, based on the presence of excessive body fat and adverse effects on health (mortality and morbidity) as follows:

Category	BMI (kg/m^2)	Risk of co-morbidities*
Underweight	<18.5	Low**
Normal range	18.5 to 24.9	Average
Overweight	> or = 25.0	
Pre-Obese	25.0 to 29.9	Increased
Obese class I	30.0 to 34.9	Moderate
Obese class II	35.0 to 39.9	Severe
Obese class III	>or = 40.0	Very severe

*E.g., high blood pressure, diabetes mellitus, high cholesterol.
** However, risk of other medical problems are increased.

The BMI definitions are not valid in children, the elderly, athletic or muscular individuals, and pregnant or lactating women.

Recent studies demonstrated that Asians have higher levels of body fat percentage compared to age- and sex-matched Caucasians with the same BMI and have higher prevalence of risk factors for heart and blood vessel disease at levels of BMI considered to be normal by the WHO.

Therefore a new Classification for Asian Adults according to BMI (awaiting ratification by the WHO in late 2003) has been proposed. The cut-off BMI for overweight has been reduced to 23 from 25 and for obesity has been reduced to 27.5 from 30.

Abdominal obesity

Excessive accumulation of body fat in the abdominal region (abdominal adiposity) is associated with risk factors of heart disease which include type 2 diabetes mellitus, high blood pressure, high blood cholesterol and is an independent predictor of morbidity. A simple and practical way of assessing abdominal fat is the use of waist circumference.

Thresholds for high-risk gender-specific waist measurement are as follows:

Guidelines	Waist circumference (cm)	
	Men	Women
WHO	102	88
Asians	90	80

Health risks of overweight (BMI >or=25)

Obesity is associated with various chronic diseases which include type 2 diabetes mellitus, high blood pressure, high blood cholesterol, heart disease, strokes, sleep apnea, arthritis and certain forms of cancer. This has led to increased health care costs, both for the individuals and the nation. It has led to significant emotional suffering as a consequence of discrimination in a society that places great emphasis on physical appearance. Life-span is also reduced mainly from heart and blood vessel diseases.

Health risks of underweight (BMI <18.5)

In affluent Singapore where food is plentiful, the health risks of being underweight are relatively unknown to Singaporeans until the Slim 10 incident surfaced in early 2002. Several media reports subsequently highlighted the widespread use of prescription slimming medications and OTC slimming products among our young female population many of whom were not overweight by the criteria detailed above. A small proportion of this population may be suffering from some form of eating disorders (e.g., anorexia nervosa and bulimia nervosa). The prevalence of anorexia nervosa in young women has been estimated to be about 0.5% to 1% and from 1% to 3% for bulimia nervosa.

Anorexia nervosa is characterised by a fixed, distorted body image and attitude towards eating and weight, involving hoarding of food and enjoyment of weight loss (to at least 15% below their expected body weight) and cessation of menstruation. Other characteristics of anorexia nervosa include fear of fatness, food restriction through reduced intake and ritualised exercise.

Individuals with **bulimia nervosa** are usually within the normal weight range though they often have rapid fluctuations in weight. They have chaotic eating habits and exercise weight control through vomiting with binge eating. Ritualised exercise is rarely seen in the bulimic patients.

Individuals with eating disorders described above will need psychiatric treatment. Although no survey has been done, a significant proportion of our population (particularly the young females) who took slimming medications and OTC slimming products most probably did not suffer from eating disorders as described above but were influenced by culturally driven attitudes and beliefs, especially in a society that places great emphasis on physical appearance. The yearning to be thinner was compounded by advertisements, with media glorifying people who were underweight and medically unhealthy. Normal-sized girls looked up to dangerously thin models as having the "to-die-for" physique. The adverse effects on health experienced by this group of individuals will depend on the degree and rapidity of the weight loss and the adverse effects of the slimming products taken as exemplified by the Slim 10 incident. The adverse effects of the various slimming products (prescription and OTC) have been extensively covered by media reports after the Slim 10 incident. Too rapid weight loss, i.e., more than two kilograms per week may result in heart problems and can cause death due to heart failure. As an individual dropped from normal weight into the underweight range, he or she becomes more susceptible to certain diseases which include osteoporosis, cessation of menstruation and infertility. Their immunity is compromised and their resistance to infection is very much reduced.

Several diseases such as tuberculosis, HIV, diabetes mellitus, hyperthyroidism (increased activity of the thyroid), malabsorption syndromes (where the guts have problems absorbing nutrients) are associated with weight loss and hence underweight.

OTC (Over-The-Counter) slimming products

There is no scientific evidence to show that current OTC slimming products are effective. It is difficult to determine the nature and action of the ingredients from labels of OTC slimming products, as a lot of these ingredients are herbal preparations and we do not know their actions and side effects. Slim 10 was first introduced to Singaporeans in November 2001 as an OTC slimming product. It has subsequently been found to be adulterated with two undeclared ingredients, namely nicotinamide and Fenfluramine, a slimming drug. The sale of fenfluramine was banned in 1997 when it was found to cause heart valve disorders and heart failure especially when used in combination with another slimming agent, phentermine. Certain OTC slimming products contain unsafe ingredients. Ephedrine is sometimes misleadingly labelled with its herbal names of ma huang or ephedra, while caffeine can be listed as guarana or kola nut. They have caused nervousness, dizziness, altered blood pressure and heart rate and in serious cases, heart attack, stroke, seizures and even death. Another popular slimming product contains chromium picolinate, a trace element touted to be able to reduce weight. When taken in big doses, i.e., six to 12 times the recommended daily allowance, chromium picolinate can lead to blood disorders such as anaemia, impairment of liver and kidney function.

Safe and effective slimming

The Slim 10 incident has demonstrated the risks of medically unsupervised slimming and the taking of OTC slimming products. As discussed above, it is very important to first establish that there is an overweight problem. Once this is established, the individual should have a baseline physical examination with appropriate laboratory investigations to detect any associated medical problems which should be treated. Secondary causes of obesity (comprising < 5% in most series) such as drug-induced obesity with steroids and hormonal disorders such as hypothyroidism, hypogonadism and Cushing's disease must be excluded first before starting a weight loss programme.

A good weight loss programme should be medically supervised and should include dietary counselling, exercise and behavioural therapy as its pillars. Slimming medications are prescribed only if the weight loss goals are not attained usually after a period of three months. They are prescribed for a limited period only because of their side-effects. Surgery such as Laparoscopic Banding of the stomach is reserved for the morbidly obese. Liposuction is useful for removing unsightly collections of fat after attaining normal BMI. Subsequent to the weight loss programme, there should be a weight maintenance programme for participants who have attained their weight loss goals.

It is not advisable and may even be dangerous to take up a weight loss programme, use a fat loss technique, or consume an OTC slimming product which has not been scientifically proven to be effective and safe.

Prescription slimming drugs

The following drugs are approved for use in the treatment of obesity in Singapore. They must be prescribed and supervised by a doctor. They are used as adjunct to diet and exercise for the obese individuals and those who are overweight with risk factors such as diabetes mellitus and high blood cholesterol levels. They should not be taken by individuals below 18 years of age and women who are pregnant or breastfeeding.

Orlistat (Brand Name: Xenical)
It acts as a fat-blocker. It blocks 30% of the ingested fat in food from being absorbed. When used correctly, it can bring about substantial weight loss and has the potential to change an individual's perception of fatty and oily foods.

Sibutramine (Brand Name: Reductil)
It is a satiety enhancer. It is taken once daily and reduces food intake by bringing about the early "feeling of fullness", resulting in weight loss.

Phentermine (Brand Names: Panbesy, Duromin, Ionamin, Umine)

D-Norpseudoephedrine (Brand Name: Mirapront N)

Mazindol (Brand Name: Teronac)

These three drugs are appetite suppressants. Because of their adverse side-effects and rebound weight gain which can be quite severe on cessation of ingestion, they are rarely prescribed.

Prevention

Born into a food paradise like Singapore and a society that places great emphasis on physical appearance, Singaporeans especially the women are in a dilemma in the management of our body weights. However we must realise that it is very important to maintain our weight in the normal range. Steering our body weight to either side of the normal range (i.e., overweight or underweight) will jeopardise our health. There is no short-cut to weight loss and the best treatment is prevention by leading a healthy lifestyle consisting of moderation in dietary intake and daily exercise throughout life. Towards this end, public education has an important role to play. Dissemination of scientific, evidence-based knowledge on obesity and its treatment through regular public forums, the media (newspapers, magazines, television and radio broadcasts), schools and work places can help to clear up the public's myths and misconceptions on obesity and obesity treatment and for our young female population who are normal weight, to have a proper perspective on their body image (shape and size) in relationship to their body health.

Conclusion

I have highlighted the eating disorders including anorexia nervosa, misconceptions on obesity and weight management in our population. I have detailed the definitions of obesity, discussed the health risks of being overweight and underweight, the risks and dangers of unsupervised slimming and the taking of OTC slimming products. I have emphasised the role of public health education in the prevention of obesity and the correction of misconceptions on obesity and weight management.

References

A C Nielsen. *Survey on Perceptions among Singaporeans on Obesity and Weight Management. The New Paper*, 20 August 2003 and *Today*, 21 August 2003.

World Health Organisation. Obesity: Preventing and Managing the Global Epidemic. Report on a WHO consultation on obesity. Geneva, 3–5 June 1997. WHO/NUT/NCD/98.1. Geneva, 1998.

The Genetic Basis of Obesity

Lim Tit Meng
Associate Professor
Vice-Dean
Department of Biological Sciences
Faculty of Science
National University of Singapore

What is obesity?

Obesity is defined as being more than 20% over an ideal weight of a person appropriate for a certain age group, height and gender. It is a major risk factor for diabetes, heart disease, high blood pressure, stroke, gallstones as well as some cancers and forms of arthritis. People with a Body Mass Index (measure of weight relative to height) of 25 to 29.9 are overweight. A Body Mass Index of 30 or more indicates obesity.

SLIM Chance FAT Hope

Why am I born to be fat?

Some people wonder why they never seemed to be able to shed their excess body fat despite dietary control, exercising, or going through a sliming regime. To make them feel worse, they may have friends who seemed to have the innate ability to burn up excess calories with ease even if they indulge in fatty food and never exercise. They may question if they are born to be fat.

The answer to the question may not be too encouraging for some fat people. In fact, recent scientific studies have confirmed that there are genes that will make people more prone to being fat. Some people are indeed born with the tendency to become obese. To these people it may well be legitimate for them to blame their genes for being obese.

What is a gene?

All of us, like any living thing on earth, are under our own genetic definition. The genetic make-up of an individual predisposes a person to a certain physical trait. The type of genes will affect the type of outward appearance of a person. In biological terms, it means genotype defines phenotype.

A gene is a stretch of DNA (deoxyribonucleic acid) sequence in the chromosome that codes for an instruction to make a gene product, usually in the form of a protein molecule. Proteins are one of the basic building blocks for making a cell. Proteins are also a major part of the cell's machinery that enable its live functions such as respiration, storage of energy, growth and death. Hence genes are very important for proper physiology to take place in our body. If a gene is mutated even by a single frameshift (meaning the DNA sequence is shifted by one nucleotide base compared to the normal gene), the gene product may be severely affected. The defect may have a bearing on the physiology. The physiology will in turn affect our physical wellness including our body weight.

Genes do not act alone. Often the environmental conditions and factors can either help to express or suppress a gene. To a large extent our physiological and physical state are the combined outcome of genetic and environmental controls. While some of our health status can be due to extrinsic factors, and extrinsic factors can sometimes override the intrinsic genetic influence, some of our bodily conditions are solely the effect of genetic predisposition.

Fat deposition is one of our biological functions that form part of our normal physiology. Excess energy through food intake can be converted into fat and stored in the body as fat cells that make the adipose tissues (such as the fat layer under the skin). Fat storage is a survival adaptation in an animal to prepare it for a time of starvation or for winter hibernation when fat can be burned through respiratory reaction to release energy needed to sustain life.

Human beings do not hibernate but we do have the physiological mechanisms to convert excess energy into fat storage. Our body constantly deals with energy intake and energy expenditure. Energy balance is a highly regulated process in physiology. This physiological process is facilitated through chemicals. The chemicals are in the form of enzymes, hormones and neuropeptides. These chemicals are mainly protein in nature and they operate in our body involving the digestive system and the nervous system. These proteins are the product of genes and some of these genes when mutated will result in excess fat storage, if their gene products disrupt the balance between energy intake and expenditure, leading to obesity. Such genes are generally called obesity genes.

Sadly, some people inherit these obesity genes that make them grow fatter then desired!

What are the experimental proofs that obesity has a genetic basis?

While health experts emphasise that improved diets and increased physical activity could solve the problem of obesity, scientists have shown evidence that genetics play a large part in the development of obesity.

To understand the physiology behind the obesity genes, we should first look back at some experiments conducted in the 1950s–1960s using parabiotic mice. Parabiotic mice are a pair of mice with their blood circulation united by surgical means. The experimental technique of parabiosis involves making an incision along the lateral aspect of two animals, then suturing them together to allow exchange of blood-borne molecules. Parabiosis means these animals have parallel biological functions since they share one blood circulation. Such an experimental procedure is now a rare practice. However, in the 1950s and 1960s before molecular biology tools were available, parabiotic experiments allow the analysis of why some mice were obese and some were slim from a general physiological perspective.

The experiments involved one genetic strain of mice known as the *ob* (obese) mouse, another known as *db* (diabetic) mouse, and the normal mouse. The *ob* and *db* mice are all obese in size, while the normal mice given normal diet are normal in weight. Parabiotic pairs were constructed between *ob*, *db* and normal mice and their body weight measured over time. The results were very interesting.

Experiment A: When an obese *ob* mouse was surgically paired with a normal mouse, the *ob* mouse lost weight.

Experiment B: When an obese *db* mouse was paired with a normal mouse, the normal mouse stopped eating and lost weight.

Experiment C: When an obese *ob* mouse was surgically paired with an obese *db* mouse, the *ob* mouse stopped eating and lost weight, whereas the *db* mouse was unaffected.

The experiments are schematically illustrated in the following cartoon:

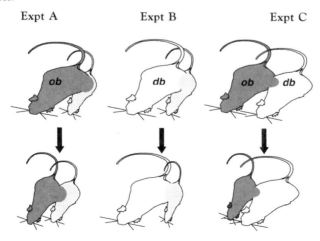

Expt A   Expt B   Expt C

The results gave rise to the following conclusions:

(1) There is something in the normal mouse blood that can cause the *ob* mouse to lose weight.

(2) The *ob* and *db* mice are genetically different since the *ob* mouse but not the *db* mouse lost weight after surgically paired with the normal mouse.

(3) The *db* mouse blood has something that causes weight loss in *ob* mouse, but the *ob* mouse blood does not contain something that can cause weight loss in *db* mouse.

(4) That something is a factor that can control body weight. The normal mouse blood has this factor, the *db* mouse has it, but the *ob* mouse lacks it.

An additional experiment was conducted with two normal mice surgically paired and one of them was overfed prior to parabiosis. The result was that the overfed twin partner lost weight.

Taken together, the observations were consistent with the idea that there exists a satiety hormone, presumably the *ob* gene product, which is produced in the normal mouse. The *ob* mouse has the mutated *ob* gene such that this hormone is not produced or is defective. When the parabiotic normal mouse blood circulated the normal hormone to the *ob* mouse, the *ob* mouse stopped eating and lost weight.

In physiology, a protein as a hormone will always have a receptor for it. *The hormone circulates in the blood, and cells with the appropriate receptor will respond to the hormone and the hormonal effect manifests.* The receptor is often a protein that sits on the cell surface. Like hormones, their receptors are also the product of genes.

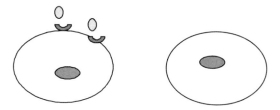

The cell on the left with membrane receptors (⌣) for a hormone (○) will respond to the hormonal signal when the hormone binds to the receptor. The cell on the right without the receptor will not respond to the hormone. The response involves turning on/off genes inside the cell nucleus (⬭).

The *db* gene product was assumed to be the receptor that can bind the satiety hormone produced by the *ob* gene. In the *db* mutant mouse, the receptor is lacking or defective. Even when its blood contains the satiety hormone, the body could not respond to its signal. This assumption could explain why when the *ob* mouse was surgically paired with *db* mouse, the *ob* mouse lost weight. The *db* mouse will have normal *ob* gene product that codes for the satiety hormone, and the hormone from the *db* mouse will restore the deficiency of this hormone in the *ob* mouse.

However, the *db* mouse has a deficiency in the satiety hormone receptor, and pairing with the *ob* mouse with deficiency in the hormone further complicates the deficiency in weight control. Hence the *db* mouse surgically paired with the *ob* mouse remained obese.

In the case of parabiotic normal mice experiment, the satiety hormone and receptors are all normal in the mice. When one was overfed, the satiety hormone circulated in both mice and made the other twin mouse stop eating and lost weight.

The above conclusions are consistent with the theory of a "lipostat" mechanism. According to the "lipostatic theory", an individual has an "ideal fat content" where this level is maintained even if fat cells are removed or added surgically. The lipostat controls food intake and metabolism and aims to maintain energy balance to keep the ideal fat content in our body. The satiety hormone would then be the effector of the "lipostat".

The *ob* and *db* genes were finally cloned in the 1990s, and they gave strong support to the hypotheses derived from the parabiotic experiments done in the 1960s. The *ob* gene encodes the hormone leptin and the *db* gene the leptin receptor. Leptin is secreted by fat cells and has dual activity of decreasing food intake and increasing metabolic rate, which makes the old "lipostatic theory" for control of food intake very appealing.

When *ob* mice are treated with injections of leptin they lose their excess fat and return to normal body weight. In contrast, leptin injection had no effect on the *db* mice. The failure of leptin to reduce body weight or food intake in *db* mice is consistent with earlier suggestions that these mutant mice lack the leptin receptor and are thus not responding to the effects of the leptin hormone.

The leptin legacy

Leptin was discovered in 1994 by Dr. Jeffrey Friedman at the Rockefeller University. The leptin receptor was cloned in 1995–1996 by other groups of scientists. Leptin came from the Greek word *leptos*, meaning thin. It is produced by fat cells and secreted into the bloodstream, where it travels to the brain and other tissues, causing fat loss and decreased appetite. Leptin signals the brain that plenty of fat is present. The brain then shuts down the appetite when enough leptin (meaning enough fat) is present. Leptin receptors are highly expressed in areas of the hypothalamus in the brain, which are known to be important in regulating body weight. Leptin's effects on body weight are mediated through effects on hypothalamic centres that control feeding behaviour and hunger, body temperature and energy expenditure. In essence, leptin provides the body with an index of nutritional status.

The relationship of leptin level and fat content through the regulation of food intake and energy expenditure is demonstrated as follows:

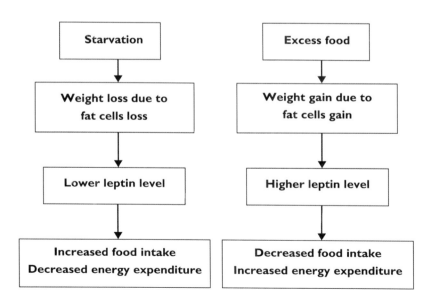

Soon after the discovery of leptin, there was hope and hype about whether it would lead to a magic bullet solution to solve obesity. Overnight the *ob* gene became the world's first celebrity gene, frequently mentioned in popular publications such as *Newsweek*, *Time* and *The Wall Street Journal*. Some drug companies even invested millions of dollars with the intension of developing leptin-based anti-obesity drugs.

Subsequently, leptin was tested in some clinical cases. The 16 September 1999 issue of *The New England Journal of Medicine* reported the results of a year-long trial of genetically engineered recombinant leptin in a 9-year-old girl who was homozygous (meaning the same gene was in both her paternal and maternal sets of chromosomes) for a frameshift mutation in her leptin genes. Her genetic condition made her lack in the leptin hormone, resulting in obesity. She began the trial weighing 94.4 kg, of which 55.9 kg was fat. She was given daily injections of recombinant leptin for one year. At the end of the treatment, she had lost 16.4 kg, most of it fat. Her appetite and thus food intake had decreased. This report seemed to spell some hope in anti-obesity treatment.

However, as clinical trials progressed, leptin was not looking to be quite as effective as first thought. The hormone had been effective only in the 5% of obese people who lacked the ability to make leptin. Otherwise, for the vast majority of the obese people, the hormone had been largely ineffective in reducing weight. In fact, because fat cells produce leptin, most obese people would have high levels of the hormone intrinsically.

Soon scientists came to realise that the highly touted hormone leptin goes only part of the way in treating obesity, because the hormone works solely by curbing appetite. It is now recognised that the physiology of obesity is complex with many different pathways involved. The discovery of leptin although did not lead to the magic bullet solution for obesity, it initiated a worldwide effort in understanding the molecular mechanisms of weight control. In the past few years, more genes have been identified to play a role in the regulation of food intake, body weight and obesity. The discoveries of many scientists are now piecing together the intricate pathways.

Interplay of genes that affect the physiological pathways in obesity

There are three type of genes related to three pathways leading to obesity: (a) satiety or feeding control genes that can affect appetite and hence food intake; (b) thermiogenesis or heat generating genes that can lead to burning off excess energy and hence lower fat storage; (c) adipogenesis or fat cells making genes that will convert body cells into fat cells.

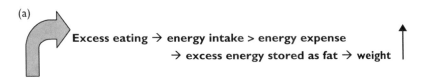

(a) **Excess eating → energy intake > energy expense → excess energy stored as fat → weight**

Big appetite (feeding behaviour controlled by the hypothalamus in our brain)

(b) **Energy stored in cells** **Burn off as heat** **→ Reduced fat storage**

(c)

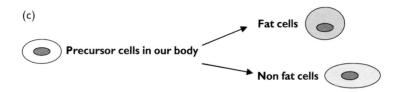

It gradually became clear that leptin and its receptor are only two of what may turn out to be a large number of genes that are important in the control of body weight and obesity. Some of the other satiety or feeding control genes and gene products involved in control of food intake and body weight include the following. It is interesting to note that they are somehow inter-related in their mode of operation.

Neuropeptide Y is a hormone synthesised in many areas of the brain and also secreted from the gut. It is a potent stimulator of feeding behaviour. Leptin appears to suppress feeding in part by inhibiting expression of neuropeptide Y.

Melanocortins exert their effect certain in brain hypothalamic neurons and inhibit feeding behaviour. Targeted disruptions of a melanocortin receptor in mice are associated with development of obesity. It was also recently shown that one of the melanocortins, known as the alpha-melanocyte-stimulating hormone (**alpha-MSH**), can reduce weight gain in both genetic and diet-induced obese mice when it was administered to them. The alpha-MSH has the opposite effect of neuropeptide Y.

Ghrelin is an appetite stimulatory signal from the stomach. The gut hormones ghrelin, like neuropeptide Y, is secreted from the gut in response to changes to nutritional status. A rare genetic disease known as the Prader–Willi syndrome is an inherited condition that causes its victim to be extremely obese. These victims have a very high level of ghrelin although the increased ghrelin production is apparently an indirect effect of the other chromosomal abnormalities underlying the disease. Interestingly, ghrelin production has been found to increase in people who had lost weight through dieting. The hormone may thus be responsible for undermining a dieter's ability to lose weight.

Cholecystokinin (CCK) is another neuropeptide released from the gut in response to food intake. It works through the CCK receptors in the brain and in the gut to trigger a feeling of satiety.

Beacon is a newly discovered gene. It has variations, or mutated forms, that are associated with the onset of obesity and fat deposit around the waist. The beacon gene is expressed in the hypothalamus of the brain and is associated with overeating. It may stimulate food intake by activating the neuropeptide Y.

Carboxypeptidase E (*fat* gene) is the enzyme necessary for proteolytic processing, a chemical step in activation of proinsulin and perhaps other hormones such as neuropeptide Y. Mice with mutations in this gene gradually become obese as they age, and develop hyperglycemia with high sugar level in the blood. The high sugar level can be suppressed by treatment with insulin. Insulin deficiency leads to diabetes and diabetes is often associated with obesity. When the carbixypeptidase E is deficient in converting proinsulin into active insulin, obesity sets in.

Tubby protein, along with tubby-related proteins, are presumed transcription factors which can turn on other genes. Tubby protein is highly expressed in the paraventricular nucleus of the hypothalamus and other regions of the brain. Mice with mutations in the tubby gene show adult onset of obesity, but the mechanisms involved are not known.

The following are genes or gene products involved in thermiogenesis or heat generating process. The process affects the energy balance in our body and hence has an impact on weight control.

The **cannabinoid receptor type 1 (CB1)** and its endogenous ligands (proteins that the receptor can bind to), the endocannabinoids, are involved in the regulation of food intake. The cannabinoid system is an essential endogenous regulator of energy balance in our body.

Mitochondrial uncoupling proteins are proteins present inside the cellular sub-structure called mitochondria where cellular respiration actually takes place to generate energy. They were first discovered in brown fat, and subsequently identified in white fat and muscle cells. They allow mitochondria within those cells to uncouple a chemical process known as oxidative phosphorylation, for generating heat. They may play an important role in energy expenditure and thus in body weight control.

Beta-adrenergic receptors are present on brown fat and perhaps white fat. Binding of norepinephrine (a hormone related to stress) to this receptor on fat cells leads to increased transcription (a process of turning on genes) of the mitochondrial uncoupling protein, allowing increased heat production via hydrolysis (a chemical process of breaking down molecules) of fatty acids. It was recently reported that certain mutations in this gene predisposed people to become obese and develop diabetes before middle age.

The third class of genes related to obesity is the adipogenesis or fat cells making genes. Scientists have recently found a genetic switch which controls the formation of fat cells in mice. If the switch is on, fat cells will not develop. If it is off, even would-be muscles cells turn to fat. The fat switch has been identified as a class of proteins known as **Wnts** (pronounced "wints"). In the absence of Wnt, both precursor muscle cells and precursor fat cells consistently differentiated into fat cells.

Wnts are well known for regulating the complex genetic and biochemical changes that take place during embryological development. When Wnt protein binds to a cell membrane receptor, it sets off a chain of biochemical signals which eventually reach the cell nucleus and either turn on or off genes that regulate development.

Recent findings show that two fat-making transcription factors inside the cell nucleus produce genetic commands for transforming would-be fat cells into fat cells. Normally, Wnt signaling seems to inhibit these factors. When the cellular signal is turned off, however, the transcription factors are free to make pre-fat cells balloon. Even pre-muscle cells also can turn into fat if Wnt signaling is turned off.

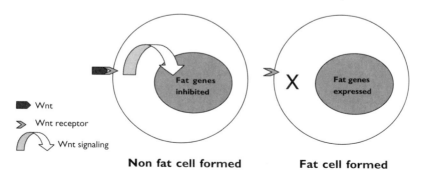

Wnt

Wnt receptor

Wnt signaling

Fat genes inhibited

Fat genes expressed

Non fat cell formed   **Fat cell formed**

Obesity is therefore a multifactoral and polygenic problem

The discovery of obesity genes and their inter-relationship in the physiological pathways that affect food intake, body weight and fat content has allow us a deeper insight into the complexity of energy balance and obesity. We now understand that obesity can occur as a result of genetic or acquired changes in three main types of biochemical processes.

The feeding control genes will determine the sensations of satiety and hunger through processes that depend on the interplay between internal signals (notably leptin) and environmental factors. Another set of genes affect energy efficiency in our body through the activation of heat generating processes to dissipate part of the energy contained in food as heat instead of accumulating it as fat. The third set of genes control adipogenesis, the process by which cells specialised in fat storage are formed. This is controlled by the interplay of transcription factors that lead to the switch for fat cell formation.

The knowledge of the growing number of genes implicated in these three types of processes and of their inter-relationships is leading toward a molecular genetic understanding of the body weight regulatory system. This knowledge is paving the way for new methods of obesity control. Several anti-obesity compounds are now in the pipeline either in preclinical or various stages of clinical development.

Fat chance and slim hope

Besides finding cures or management strategies to deal with obesity and weight control, an additional motivation to unlock the mystery of obesity genes lies in the fact that leanness may well be the key to longevity. Many experiments have shown that caloric restriction by means of dietary control can extend the life span of organisms ranging from the flies to mice. A recent work showed that when mice were genetically modified such that their fat cells did not make the insulin receptors, they had 50% to 70% less fat than the normal mice. Not only did they appear healthy, their average life span also increased from 30 months to 33.5 months. These genetically modified mice actually ate more than the normal mice but they did not produce more fat cells as a result. By staying slim, while enjoying food, each of these mice could still hopefully live longer than the normal mice.

While researching on genes that make us fat, one fine day we might chance upon the secret to longevity. Hopefully that day will come soon!

References arranged in chronological order for tracing of major obesity genes studied

Martin RJ, White BD, Hulsey MG. The regulation of body weight. *Amer Scientist* **79**:528–541. 1991. [review of parabiosis experiments and control of food intake in general]

Zhang Y, Proenca R, Maffei M, Barone M, Leopold L, Friedman JM. Positional cloning of the mouse obese gene and its human homologues. *Nature*, **372**:425–432. 1994.

Ghilardi N, Ziegler S, Wiestner A, Stoffel R, Heim MH, Skoda RC. Defective STAT signaling by the leptin receptor in diabetic mice. *Proc Natl Acad Sci* **93**:6231–6235. 1996.

Wolf G. A new uncoupling protein: A potential component of the human body weight regulation system. *Nutrition Reviews* **55**:178. 1997.

Comuzzie AG and Allison DB. The search for human obesity genes. *Science* **280**:1374–1377. 1998.

Friedman JM, Halaas JL. Leptin and the regulation of body weight in mammals. *Nature* **395**:763. 1998.

Gura T. Uncoupling proteins provide new clue to obesity's causes. *Science* **280**:1369–1370. 1998.

Marsh DJ, Hollopeter G, Kafer KE, Palmiter RD. Role of the Y5 neuropeptide Y receptor in feeding and obesity. *Nat Med* **4**:718–721. 1998.

Woods SC, Seeley RJ, Porte D, Schwartz MW. Signals that regulate food intake and energy homeostasis. *Science* **280**:1378–1383. 1998.

Tritos NA, Maratos-Flier E. Two important systems in energy homeostasis: Melanocortins and melanin-concentrating hormone. *Neuropeptides* **33**(5):339–349. 1999.

Benoit SC, Schwartz MW, Lachey JL *et al.* A novel selective melanocortin-4 receptor agonist reduces food intake in rats and mice without producing adverse consequences. *J Neurosci* **20**:3442–3448. 2000.

Mertens IL, Van Gaal LF. Promising new approaches to the management of obesity. *Drugs* **60**(1):1–9. 2000.

Palou A, Serra F, Bonet ML, Pico C. Obesity: Molecular bases of a multifactorial problem. *Eur J Nutr* **39**(4):127–144. 2000.

Ross S *et al*. Inhibition of adipogenesis by Wnt signaling. *Science* **289**: 950–953. 2000.

Walder K, McMillan JS, Lee S, Civitarese A, Zimmet P, Collier GR. Effects of beacon administration on energy expenditure and substrate utilisation in *Psammomys obesus* (Israeli sand rats). *Int J Obes Relat Metab Disord* **25**(9):1281–1285. 2001.

Santagata S, Boggon TJ, Baird CL, *et al*. G-protein signaling through tubby proteins. *Science* **292**:2041–2050. 2001.

Clement K, Boutin P, Froguel P. Genetics of obesity. *Am J Pharmacogenomics* **2**(3):177–187. 2002.

Hofbauer KG. Molecular pathways to obesity. *Int J Obes Relat Metab Disord* **26** Suppl 2:S18–27. 2002.

Asakawa A, Inui A, Kaga T, Katsuura G, Fujimiya M, Fujino MA, Kasuga M. Antagonism of ghrelin receptor reduces food intake and body weight gain in mice. *Gut* **52**(7):947–952. 2003.

Cota D, Marsicano G, Tschöp M, Grübler Y, Flachskamm C, Schubert M, Auer D, Yassouridis A, Thöne-Reineke C, Ortmann S, Tomassoni F, Cervino C, Nisoli E, Linthorst ACE, Pasquali R, Lutz B, Stalla GK, Pagotto U. The endogenous cannabinoid system affects energy balance via central orexigenic drive and peripheral lipogenesis. *J Clin Invest* **112**(3):423–431. 2003.

Donnelly R. Researching new treatments for obesity: from neuroscience to inflammation. *Diabetes, Obesity and Metabolism* **5**:1–4. 2003.

Liu YJ, Araujo S, Recker RR, Deng HW. Molecular and genetic mechanisms of obesity: Implications for future management. *Curr Mol Med* **3**(4):325–40. 2003.

Marx J. Cellular warriors at the battle of the bulge. *Science* **299**: 846–849. 2003.

Neary NM, Small CJ, Bloom SR. Gut and mind. *Gut* **52**(7):918–921. 2003.

Slim 10:
Fat Hopes?

Dr. Daniel Fung
*Consultant Psychiatrist and Deputy Chief
Department of Child and Adolescent Psychiatry
Institute of Mental Health*

T he furore following the Slim 10 controversy ranged from blaming the Health Sciences Authority (HSA) for not keeping the country safe from banned substances to the rights of organ transplant recipients and the sanctity of saving life over rules and regulations. Yet there has been little discussion over the important issue about a woman's relentless pursuit of thinness and the social perception of beauty.

Why is the perception of thinness becoming prevalent?

The concern for thinness is becoming more than just an overvalued idea. I would like to draw attention to the issue of the underlying social psychopathology: Being thin is a preoccupation of many young (and not so young) people today. Why is it so? Not more than a few decades ago, the concept of beauty was a lady who would be, by today's anorexic standards, an overweight woman averaging more than 70 kilograms. These days, women larger than 40 kilograms may be considered too big. Perhaps it is the unending series of media ads about slim women (mostly actresses and models) who have transformed themselves from bloated balloons into bathing beauties. Just pick up any glossy magazine, even those about cars and parenting, and you will notice that slim, petite models adorn the covers. I have noticed many of my female colleagues and friends who eat miniscule amounts during mealtimes. When asked, they inevitably give three excuses, "I am not hungry", "The food isn't nice" or "I am avoiding fatty foods". Slimming is part of a larger and more sinister development that I have noticed. More young girls are seen in our clinic for unhappiness over how they look, the general dissatisfaction with who they are or what they will become. This is not even confined to girls, even boys have similar preoccupation about their outward appearance. I remember teenagers who feel their eyes are too small or the nose is too large. Slimming has become one of the panaceas for the ills of society. If I do not feel good about myself, I will just lose a few kilograms and I feel better already.

Why do people take slimming products?

The idea that slimming can change the way people feel about themselves is a powerful one. It is helped by the advertorials frequently seen in our newspapers which will have a svelte lady describe how slimming has made her the object of desire. More importantly, it sets the tone for a whole host of products that are reputed to reduce weight with the least amount of effort. Take this natural supplement, and it will reduce your need to eat. The ads scream "natural way to losing weight" or "lose kilograms without avoiding your favourite foods". The idea of a natural product or method that can reduce weight without the usual exercise or pain of dieting is too tempting an idea. This is no different from the gambler who hopes that he will make a fortune at the next roll of the die.

What about medical slimming?

The slimming industry has grown to considerable size. It has enlisted the help of medical professionals in the light of health warnings about obesity and for the obvious benefits of good self-esteem. Pharmacies and health shops have stocked themselves full of capsules and other substances that purport to reduce weight. Doctors have not helped the matter. When I was in Toronto, I remembered a doctor had set up a weight control clinic. The ads emphasised the medical legitimacy of what was obviously another slimming centre cloaked in medical jargon. In Singapore, we have yet to see this in widespread practice but doctors are often consulted on slimming. Under the guise of the healthcare industry, weight loss has become legitimised and acceptable. But the truth of the matter is that there is no compelling scientific evidence that slimming aids such as Chitosan or even herbal teas have any real function in making a person slim beyond just reducing their hunger and need to eat.

What is the good doctor's advice?

If you are seeking medical advice on slimming, good doctors often respond to what is in the best interest of the patient. It is responsibility of the doctor to educate patients about the need for a healthy diet rather than a starvation one. If a patient requests for slimming, it behoves the doctor to identify the reasons behind these, including self-esteem, issues. If the issue of looking good is an overwhelming preoccupation, some education on the dangers of this can be highlighted. In the development of eating disorders, it often starts as a misconceived belief that being thin makes one beautiful. This is patently untrue and doctors can help their patients feel good about themselves by getting them to identify the positive aspects of their lives. Doctors can also alert family members to the warning signs of anorexia nervosa and other eating disorders. One of my colleagues who specialises in eating disorders often explains how starvation leads to poorer brain function. This may actually be the real reason for the term "dumb blonde". I used to think that hair colouring and long straight hair was cute because you see it occasionally. Today, it is probably cute to see black hair that has not been rebonded. Good doctors do not facilitate and perpetuate the myth for the relentless pursuit of slimness. I believe that doctors have a responsibility in educating the public on what is good personal health and this includes good mental health.

What is a healthy lifestyle?

Let us use the Slim 10 episode to refocus ourselves on what is really important. Physical health is being of the right size and weight, not too thin or too fat. The current healthy lifestyle campaign emphasises healthy weight and this is important in the light of increased fattening food intake and a sedentary lifestyle. The emphasis here is to prevent physical illness. But mental health is also equally important. Mental health is being happy with who we are. The movie "Shallow Hal" starring Gwyneth Paltrow, is both funny and enlightening because it focuses on inner beauty as its core value. Such values about inner beauty starts when people are young. We need to let young girls and teens know that beauty is beyond what they see in the media. Children look to adults for an example to follow. So remember the next time you decide to skip a meal to keep your weight down, choose to eat the meal and exercise regularly instead. Remember that the children are watching. This is the responsibility of all adults, especially parents and teachers.

What is Anorexia Nervosa?

Anorexia nervosa is an illness that occurs mainly in young girls and women but may also happen to men. It is characterised by a terrifying fear of being fat and the belief is so strong that the sufferer will think that they are fat even though they are well below acceptable weight ranges. The problem is not about weight and food but the use of weight and food to deal with emotional problems. Here are some warning signs of anorexia nervosa:

- Deliberate self-starvation with weight loss
- Fear of gaining weight
- Refusal to eat
- Denial of hunger
- Constant exercising
- Greater amounts of hair on the body or the face
- Sensitivity to cold temperatures
- Absent or irregular periods
- Loss of scalp hair
- A self-perception of being fat when the person is really too thin

In situations like this, specialist help from a psychiatrist may be necessary.

Fat
Hopes

Dr. Ken Ung Eng Khean

Consultant Psychiatrist & Clinical Director
Department of Psychological Medicine, NUH
Clinical Senior Lecturer
Faculty of Medicine, NUS
Adjunct Associate Professor
Psychological Studies Academic Group, NIE/NTU

"**I** have always been repelled by fat women. I find them disgusting: their absurd sidewise waddle, their absence of body contour — breasts, laps, buttocks, shoulders, jawlines, cheekbones, *everything*, everything I like to see in a woman, obscured in an avalanche of flesh. And I hate their clothes — the shapeless, baggy dresses or, worse, the stiff elephantine blue jeans with the barrel thighs. How dare they impose that body on the rest of us?"

Love's Executioner & Other Tales of Psychotherapy, Irvin Yalom[1]

---

[1] Yalom I. *Love's Executioner and Other Tales of Psychotherapy*. Basic Books, New York, 1989.

SLIM Chance FAT Hope

The desire to lose weight drives many a sensible woman to desperate measures that smack of self-abuse and border on the irrational. To understand the relentless pursuit of thinness, one has to understand only two things. One, being fat today is an awful thing, in almost every respect. Two, being thin is "in" these days. Being thin conveys perceptions of being desired, successful and being positively thought of and approved by others. The message bombarding women, especially young ones is, "be thin and be lean" and you will be happy, successful and desirable. The bad news is that all this is partly true. The good news is that all this is only partly true. A frantic lady came to me after a talk once and stated, "Dr Ung, you must help me lose weight urgently! Tell me what to do to lose weight, my fiancé says that he will marry me only after I have lost at least 10 kilograms." I thought for a while and replied, "Forget about losing weight. Find yourself a new fiancé." This lady imagined that weight loss would transform her life — unfortunately, life is not so simple. Life often does change for the better with weight loss but not to the extent Hollywood or advertisers would have you believe. In the latest national health survey, rates of obesity have increased for Malay and Indian females, adding to their pressures to be thinner. Imaginative research that compares the average weights of *Playboy* centerfolds and Miss America contestants against the average weight of American females from 1959 to 1988 show a progressive increase in the average weight of American females and decreased weights in models and centrefolds[2]. Indeed for the young of the female human species, the difference between the desired and the actual keeps getting further and further apart. The hopes of the fat are increasingly more and more hung on thin air.

Fat people are confronted by lists of "increased risks of physical diseases" that grow longer and longer each year. Heart disease, cancer, hypertension, osteo-arthritis, diabetes and gallstones to just name a few. Even the Japan Sumo Association started fat testing for the first time in the 2000-year-old sport. Being obese today has few advantages, apart perhaps from being less likely to sustain a hip fracture (because of the cushioning of fat when you fall) and being able to survive longer in a famine (the evolutionary advantage may have been good for our overweight ancestors but certainly not for us now). The psychological "risks" are no less awful — from the obese being less likely to marry, dating less often and reporting less date satisfaction, having a greater likelihood to fall in social class on marriage, to poorer pay/remuneration, having less years of advanced education completed and being less likely to be admitted to college[3]. An expert panel consensus report concluded, "Obesity creates an enormous psychological burden. In terms of suffering, this burden may be the greatest adverse effect on obesity."[4] A review of childhood obesity

---

[2] Garner DM. Psychoeducational principles of treatment in *Handbook of Treatment for Eating Disorders*, 2nd Edition, Garner DM, Garfinkel PE (Eds). The Guildford Press, 1997.

[3] Ung EK. Psychological management of obesity. *Medical Progress* 29(4):17–25. 2002.

[4] National Institutes of Health Consensus Development Panel. Health implications of obesity. *Ann Intern Med* 103:983. 1985.

similarly states, "The most widespread consequences of childhood obesity are psychosocial."[5] Studies show children as young as six years old using derogative terms such as "lazy, stupid, ugly" to describe the silhouette of an overweight child. Doctors are not exempted from such behaviour. It is not uncommon to hear of stories where doctors have made sarcastic and cynical comments to their overweight female patients. The noted psychotherapist Irvin Yalom's quote at the beginning is probably as candid as they come. Fat kids are now enrolled in mandatory Trim and Fit (TAF) programmes. Some teachers in mandatory school weight loss programmes may be more insulting and punitive than encouraging, thus further eroding the self-esteem of their young charges (hopefully there is greater enlightenment nowadays).

The desperation to be thin has led to an explosion in advertising, products and services related to slimming and fitness. Many claim to be "proven" and by "leading authorities" (the term "European" or "Swiss" expert or centre seems to crop up with alarming regularity — perhaps because it sounds respectably "scientific"). I once actually took the effort to get information about such a "breakthough" from a "famous European centre". Not being able to find the so-called advertised "cure" in seven major recent textbooks of obesity or weight management, I turned to the Medline database (which covers all worthwhile medical research published around the world). Alas, the centre did not exist and the only

---

[5] Dietz W. Health implications of obesity in youth. *Pediatrics* **101**:518–525. 1998.

listing of someone with a similar surname to the "expert" was on research in slugs. (See a "miracle" cure you want to check for yourself. Check Medline yourself by going to the following website http://www.ncbi.nlm.nih.gov/entrez/query.fcgi?db=PubMed). Let me say it here, lest I forget — *caveat emptor* (let the buyer beware!). A new "miracle" diet is a sure bet bestseller and that there are so many such bestsellers attest to the fact that none truly work well for most! The poor overweight have to put up with miraculous photographs of "before" and "after" transformations of women visiting slimming centres that boast of the "latest" breakthrough devices and techniques, "super" fit woman flaunting their bodies in front of windows at strategic sites in the city, magazine pictures of slim models and television programmes that glamourise the slim and slender actresses and typecast overweight ones in comic roles (it is almost as if the message is that the fat should not be taken seriously). The corresponding "average" Singapore Chinese female of the same height and age range (based on weight for height reference charts for Singapore) would have a BMI of 19.5, 19.9 and 19.7 respectively. To be fair, life on the other side of the fishbowl is equally hard — a female media celebrity once confided how difficult it was to not be pressurised to be slimmer. Viewers writing in about her face being too fat and the like certainly did not go down well with her! The truth is that girls nowadays do not ask, "Is that weight going to be suitable and healthy for my body?" but "How can I look like that?"

There is a myth that "If I work really hard at it and eat right, I will end up looking like that". Truth is, there is a limit to what is achievable and some degree of acceptance is necessary. Bad genes sure is a bum deal in obesity — your risk of being obese partly depends on whether your parents are obese (80% if both parents obese, 40% if one parent obese, 14% if both parents lean). A study of 93 identical twins by Professor Albert Stunkard and his colleagues at the University of Pennsylvania found that twins who are raised in different environments often show similar patterns of weight gain. They concluded that genetic factors account for about 66% of body fatness[6]. Studies of the adopted show that adoptees are closer to their biological parent's weights then their adoptive parent's[7]. An interesting study by Claude Bouchard and his colleagues[8] looked at overfeeding in identical twins. The weight gain on the same daily intake of calories ranged from 4.3kg to 13.3kg after 84 days! Gains made by each member of a twin pair were remarkably similar. Gains made among different twin pairs were six times more variable.

Despite spending billions of dollars in efforts to slim down, Americans are fatter than ever. An estimated $33 billion is spent on weight-loss products and services by the 33% to 40% of American women and 20% to 24% men trying to lose weight

---

[6]Stunkard AJ. The body mass index of twins who have been reared apart. *New Eng J Med* **332**:1483–1487. 1990.

[7]Stunkard A *et al*. An adoption study of human obesity. *New Eng J Med* **314**:193–198. 1986. Price R *et al*. Genetic contributions to human fatness: An adoption study. *Am J Psychiatry* **144**:1003–1008. 1987.

Sorensen T *et al*. Genetics of obesity in adult adoptees and their biological siblings. *Br Med J* **298**:87–90. 1989.

[8]Bouchard C *et al*. The response of long-term overfeeding in identical twins. *New Eng J Med* **322**:1477–1482. 1990.

each year[9]. Quick to find a scapegoat and make millions of bucks in the process, Americans have turned to suing such bastions of Americanisation such as McDonald's. Although it is true that portions and servings have increased over the generations (though even McDonald's has fallen to the winds of change and begun offering more "healthy" alternatives), most experts believe that being less active is at least equally important. The irony is that despite the world telling us how good it is to be thin, all around the environment is making us fatter and fatter. Truly we live in a world that makes it so easy for us to be fat but makes it so desirable to be thin. Do people really care about all these environmental messages? It would seem very much that they do. Here are some examples — a dramatic increase in dieting and abnormal eating attitudes occurred in Fiji in the late 1990s. Women that previously considered it a status symbol to be fat suddenly started to work at losing weight, coinciding with the introduction of Western television soap operas and all those slim lithe bodies on display. In a study of pre-adolescent and adolescent schoolgirls, 69% reported that fashion and women's magazines influenced their idea of the perfect body shape and 47% wanted to lose weight because of magazine pictures[10]. Again to be fair, studies show that these do motivate women to start eating more healthily and go exercise. Watching soap operas and movies

---

[9]NIH Publication No. 96-4158, July 1996, National Institute of Diabetes and Digestive and Kidney Diseases.

[10]Becker AE, Hamburg P. Culture, the media, and eating disorders. *Harv Rev Psychiatry* **4**:163–7. 1996.

SLIM Chance FAT Hope

is positively correlated with body dissatisfaction and watching music videos, drive to thinness[11].

We can learn much from that small group of girls that takes things a bit too far and lands up with the eating disorder — anorexia nervosa. These are the true experts of weight loss — and almost every one of them gets to that "anorexic" frame by taking an ultra low fat diet (they eat almost nothing, but if they do, then it must be free of fat or oil), often coupled with intense and obsessive exercising. I have never yet come across an anorexic doing the "Atkins" (the Atkins diet is based on a low carbohydrate, "as much as you want of protein and fat" diet). Of course, that is not to say the Atkins diet does not work — two recent studies shows that it does (at least for 6–12 months and if you are one of the few that stick it out and do not drop out). It is just that it probably does not work as well for weight loss. Now is that telling us something new except that if you eat less calories and do more, you will lose weight, and that it is damned hard to keep doing this consistently — which is why anorexia is not all that common and overweight is? I guess it is not. Those with anorexia, like those who diet, can usually only hold out for so long. Like holding your breath leading to taking deep gasps of air at the end of it, restricting food usually eventually leads to bouts of overeating (and often bulimia). The anorexics' insistence on wearing apparel to maximise the display of their stick-like

[11] Tiggermann M, Pickering AS. Roke of television in adolescent women's body dissatisfaction and drive for thinness. *International Journal of Eating Disorders* 20(2):199–203. 1996.

limbs seems to be a wish to display their being "special" that mirrors the desire of most overweight females to lose weight and be "special". It is interesting that most anorexic females have to be dragged kicking and screaming into treatment and vehement protestations that "my weight is absolutely fine, there is nothing wrong with me" the rule rather than the exception. Such is the reward of being slim, that they would rather not do anything to move the status quo. Once they start bingeing and purging, that is a different story. That is often when they come back asking for help. It is as if being thin by eating a few leaves of salad a day and exercising for hours is a pretty "noble" *raison d'etre*, whereas bingeing is something quite shameful and unacceptable (and worse, it brings with it the prospect of weight gain).

It is amazing how otherwise very intelligent people fall for quick fix weight loss methods such as magnetic insoles, special rubber pants, machines that vibrate your belly and the like. This is partly due to the desperate wanting to believe in a quick fix and partly due to some really first class salesmanship and powers of persuasion that weight loss vendors have in abundance. Be clear — fast does not usually last! The way that works has to work for good, otherwise you will end up in cycles of loss and gain (some experts consider this even worse than not losing at all, though this area is still fraught with much controversy). It is not surprising that the most desperate to lose weight are women (correspondingly, female anorexics outnumber male ones 10:1). The drive to be beautiful and desirable seems to be more powerful than the drive to be fit and healthy. I once ran a weight loss group with quite a few women and only two men. It was noteworthy that almost all the women listed "wanting to look better" as a major reason for signing up and the two men listed "health concerns". At the end of the six months, the women had done better overall (with most losing weight). One man hardly lost any weight and the other did (though I suspect a lot of that loss had to do with him being knocked down by a car and ending up in hospital for some time). Fatness and overweight can be such an emotional issue for many that it blots out rational and objective thinking. In a recent study on local Chinese female undergraduates, 53% wanted to be thinner, 11.4% who were in the "underweight" range still wanted to be thinner[12]. Another local pilot study of 26 fourth year female medical students in the National University Hospital found four of ten students with BMI's below 18 reporting feeling "very fat"[13].

The Slim 10 debacle itself illustrates some of the complexities of the current "slim is in" zeitgeist and the whole slimming industry thereof. About a decade ago, the slimming pills Fenfluramine and Dex-fenfluramine were pulled off the shelf due to concerns about heart problems in a minority of sufferers. Yet it had been in use decades before and in fact the combination of Fenfluramine and Phentermine (Fen-Phen) had been touted as the hottest things in slimming only years before. The combination appears to have brought dangers to light in something that had been considered "safe" before.

---

[12] Wang MC, Ho TF, Anderson JN, Sabry ZI. Preference for thinness in Singapore — A newly industrialised society. *Singapore Med J* **40**:502–507. 1999.
[13] Ung EK, Lee DSW. Thin desires and fat realities. *Singapore Med J* **40**: 495–497. 1999.

The Food and Drug Admininstraton (FDA) of the United States — the regulatory body that monitors drugs and supplements — has been working extra hard of late to improve safeguards to slimming products. Over-the-counter and mail order supplements often contain the substance pseudo-ephedrine or its related compounds, and these have been linked to heart irregularities in a minority of those who consumed such products. The traces of Fenfluramine found in some Slim 10 samples have been touted as a possible cause of liver failure. It is difficult to monitor all such products. As they are technically not "drugs", they do not have to undergo the extensive development and testing required for drugs (which can set a pharmaceutical company back millions of dollars). It is hard to know how safe many products are (even prescription drugs, as the Fenfluramine incident illustrates) and even harder to know what works! Let us take a look at slimming salons and centres — do any of the wraps, creams, electrical devices work? No. Do people lose weight going to slimming salons and centres? Yes, some do (healthcare professionals who dismiss all such successes outright should also remind themselves that in the best university-based weight loss centres, long-term (5-year) success rates are in the order of 10–20% (worse than your chances of surviving "cancer" in general). So what is it that works? The few thousand dollars paid in advance for the "x" number of sessions help, as does everything that helps the client take in less calories (3–5 days on lemon juice and maple syrup must make you lose weight) and use up more. Clearly, if they were more open to scientific scrutiny, we would be able to learn a lot more about what can be done to maintain people's behavioural changes. In the meantime, read the small print very carefully before you sign on. I said it before and will say it again — *caveat emptor!*

Is there anything really new? What is new is: the finding that certain prescription slimming drugs and over-the-counter slimming products are more dangerous than we have thought; the discovery of various "fat" genes (despite millions of dollars of research, a genetic cure for obesity does not look imminent); new weight-reducing drugs and products; more sophisticated and informed programmes to change behaviour and thinking; the finding that severe dieting is more likely to be ineffective and dangerous; increasing understanding of the complex chemicals and systems involved in making us feel hungry and full; more information about the risks of obesity; more information about healthy eating; new surgical operations for severe obesity. In summary, there is nothing really new under the sun, only new ways of looking at the old and that the laws of physics remain true — that energy can neither be created nor destroyed, only changed from one form to another (from fat to energy for activity; and from food energy to fat). The same old truth we all know holds — take in less calories than we use up and we will lose weight, translating this simple common truth into action continues to elude the best and the brightest minds in the world. Which is where art comes into play. Weight loss is as much an art as a science and the best practitioners are those who are able to individualise what works for them and keep it up for good.

How should the health profession respond? It is futile to attempt to change societal concepts of beauty. Advertising budgets of health organisations are a mere drop in comparison with the sea of advertising funds of entertainment and corporate entities. The thin ideal is here to stay — at least for a long time. Girls just want to be thin. Girls like being thin. Men want their girls thin. Supply follows demand. Obesity is a rising problem and obesity is a genuine health hazard. Promoting healthy methods of weight control and avoiding extreme or inappropriate weight-control behaviours is a reasonable aim. Pertinent issues revolve around awareness, empowerment and promotion of healthy self-esteem. Early and wise psycho-education and intervention is likely to yield the best results. Mandatory school weight and wellness programmes should be monitored and reviewed. Teachers running such programmes would benefit from better training and support. The importance of pooling together the expertise of various disciplines to try to identify and protect those at greatest risk of developing eating disorders in such programmes cannot be overstated. Above all, we need to continue to study and monitor the safety of weight reducing products and devices and to find out what works for who and why.

To the overweight, I salute those of you who walk the walk of life with courage and grace, trying to lose weight but knowing that you are much more than what you weigh — much, much more. To the slim, I say, "You lucky - - - - - - - s". To the anorexics, I hope that you realise that you have paired up with a loser, please get help before it is too late (I have never met someone anorexic who was truly happy and a winner — maybe I am wrong, but I am still waiting to meet such a person). To those who have triumphed over obesity and eating disorder, you are the real heroes!

Legal
Perspective

True Files:

The Slim 10 Case

Raj Singam
Advocate & Solicitor, Singapore
Senior Director
Drew & Napier LLC

Introduction

"There can be no doubt that the plaintiff has undergone a life-threatening and life-changing event. In May 2002, at the age of 27, this erstwhile healthy and lively artiste was on the verge of making an untimely exit from the stage of life. A fortuitous combination of inspiring love of a selfless boyfriend, of impressive sill of a renowned surgeon and or immediate action of an enlightened Ministry of

Health, Singapore made the living donor liver transplant possible and restored the plaintiff to the world of life."

Justice Tay Yong Kwang
Andrea Heidi De Cruz v
Guangzhou Yuzhitang Health Products Co. Ltd & 4 Ors

The recent Slim 10 case where local artiste, Ms. Andrea De Cruz, successfully won damages of close to $900,000 for her injuries after a 28-day trial was one of the lawsuits that stirred up popular interest. The heart-wrenching circumstances of her injury and the ways and means of her miraculous recovery from illness featured prominently in the local media and in the hearts and minds of many Singaporeans.

The case also brought the issue of consumer protection and the rights of the consumer foremost to people's conscience. The case has brought about a welcomed awakening of the legal recourses available to everyday Singaporeans. The trial judgment has no doubt set a precedence in the field of law, in particular product liability law, locally.

We shall examine here the extraordinary circumstances of this case and explain how all of us, as consumers, are protected under the law of product liability and the legal recourses available to us if we were to ever find ourselves mired in similar circumstances.

Facts

The facts and plight of Ms. De Cruz are already well known to most people. We shall nevertheless set out in brief the facts surrounding her case.

Ms. De Cruz is an artiste in MediaCorp Studios. Sometime in December 2002, Ms. De Cruz saw TV Media's television advertisements about a slimming drug called Slim 10. The advertisements featured a "before and after" shot of MediaCorp artiste Chen Liping, highlighting Chen Liping's dramatic weight loss. These pills were represented as being 100% herbal. Convinced of the drug's effectiveness, Ms. De Cruz decided to buy Slim 10. Ms. De Cruz bought slimming pills sold and marketed in Singapore under the brand name "Slim 10" from Rayson Tan who is Chen Liping's husband and Ms. De Cruz's colleague at MediaCorp.

Sometime in the beginning of 2002, Ms. De Cruz began to consume Slim 10. Shortly after consuming the pills, Ms. De Cruz's liver failed and she came close to losing her life. Ms. De Cruz had been consuming Slim 10 for about two and a half months when she started feeling lethargic and started looking noticeably jaundiced. She was admitted into hospital. After intensive investigations, the doctors confirmed that she was suffering from drug induced massive hepatocellular necrosis with impending liver failure. Ms. Dr Cruz needed an immediate liver transplant then.

The search for a suitable donor then began. Ms. De Cruz's then boyfriend (now husband), Mr. Pierre Png was found to be a compatible donor. Ms. De Cruz underwent an adult-to-adult living donor transplant in May 2002 and was saved. Ms. De Cruz was 27 years old when her liver failed and she came very close to losing her life.

While the transplant saved Ms. De Cruz's life, she is now on lifelong medication to suppress her immune system to prevent rejection of the transplanted liver. She will continue to suffer the considerable side effects from this medication for the rest of her life.

The trial

To seek recovery for the damages suffered by her as a result of consuming Slim 10, Ms. De Cruz commenced action against the five following defendants:

(i) **Guangzhou Yuzhitang Health Products Co. Ltd.** who were the manufacturers of Slim 10. They are a company located in China. The trial against them could not continue because the process servers could not locate them in China to serve the proceedings on them.

(ii) **Health Biz Pte. Ltd.** who were the local importer of Slim 10. They were sued for negligently importing and distributing Slim 10. They were found liable.

(iii) **Semon Liu** who was the founder, director and principal shareholder of Health Biz. He was sued in his personal capacity for procuring, directing and authorising Health Biz's negligence. He was found liable.

(iv) **TV Media Pte. Ltd.** who were the sole distributor of Slim 10 in Singapore. Besides being the sole distributor, they also retailed Slim 10 directly and advertised it on television and on other media. They were sued in negligence for making untrue statements in their advertisements. They were found liable.

(v) **Rayson Tan** who was the person Ms. De Cruz bought Slim 10 from. He was sued for breach of the sale of goods contract between himself and Ms. De Cruz, in particular, for breach of the implied term that the goods sold should be of satisfactory quality. The Court found that there was no contract for the sale of goods between Ms. De Cruz and Rayson Tan because there was no intention to create legal relations. Accordingly, Rayson Tan was found not liable.

The trial was heard in the High Court of Singapore before the Honourable Justice Tay Yong Kwang. A total of 20 witnesses took the stand and gave evidence for the trial. The matter was concluded after a hearing which lasted 28 days.

The law

The law of product liability is concerned with the civil liability of manufacturers, retailers and others for damage or loss caused by defective products or products which failed to meet certain minimum standards. One of the main purposes of imposing product liability is to ensure product safety for the vulnerable ultimate consumers.

The recourses a consumer in Singapore has for product liability is an action in the tort of negligence or an action for breach of contract under the Sale of Goods Act.

What will amount to negligence will depend on the facts of each particular case. Negligence may be the omission to do something which ought to be done or the commission of something which ought to be done either in a different manner or not at all.

Ms. De Cruz succeeded against the three defendants in the tort of negligence. We shall therefore be focusing our discussion of the law of product liability on the tort of negligence.

Who is liable to the ultimate consumer — Duty of care

Under the tort of negligence, a defendant is only liable to a plaintiff if the defendant owes to that particular plaintiff a duty of care. A duty of care is a legal concept. Whether a certain class of people owe the ultimate consumer a duty to take care is determined by analogy to existing cases where similar duties have been held to exist. Therefore, the existing categories are never closed.

One of the most fundamental questions in Ms. De Cruz's case is to ask who owe a duty to her to take care to ensure Slim 10's product safety. For Ms. De Cruz's case, there have been no reported precedents in Singapore on whether, *inter alia*, the distributors, importers and the director of the importers owed a duty of care to the ultimate consumer. In this case, precedents from the United Kingdom and the United States were relied upon.

Ms. De Cruz's case has determined that, at least in Singapore, the importers and the distributors and wholesalers of the defective product would owe a duty of care to the ultimate consumer to ensure product safety.

It is interesting to note from this case that it is not necessary that the defective goods must have passed through the hands of the distributors (i.e., TV Media) for the distributors to be held liable. In this case, Ms. De Cruz did not obtain her Slim 10 pills from TV Media or from any retailers which TV Media had distributed the pills to. Ms. De Cruz instead bought her pills from Rayson Tan who obtained his pills directly from Health Biz, by-passing TV Media. TV Media were nevertheless held liable because Ms. De Cruz relied on TV Media's advertisements in deciding to buy Slim 10. The court held that TV Media, as the wholesaler which promoted, endorsed and advertised the product owed a duty to consumers to exercise reasonable care in its promotion, endorsement and advertisement.

What must be done — Standard of care

After it was determined that a duty of care was owed to Ms. De Cruz, the next question was whether the various defendants have failed to show reasonable care in the particular circumstances of the case. What is reasonable in the circumstances is a question of fact to be determined by the courts. The law lays down an objective and reasonable standard of care which has to be attained.

This case determined the standards of care that would be required from importers and distributors.

For an importer such as Health Biz, they would at least have to comply with the statutory requirements imposed for consumer safety. The court found that in this case, Health Biz failed to keep proper records of the consignment of pills that were being imported and they had failed to do proper batch tests on the pills which they were required to do under the regulatory framework.

For distributors such as TV Media, they had to take care to verify that the products that they were going to distribute were safe. They also had to ensure that what they represented to the public in their advertisements were true. The court made it clear that TV Media could not escape liability by simply saying that the wording of their advertisements was vetted and approved by the Health Sciences Authority (HSA).

It would seem that HSA's role was to merely advise, guide and facilitate the importer's compliance with the legislative framework imposed for the purpose of ensuring continued product safety. It is important to note that HSA cannot be used as a crutch for those who want to escape liability.

What went wrong — Causation

For Ms. De Cruz to succeed in her claim in negligence, not only did she have to convince the court that the defendants owed her a duty of care and that they have not met the standard of care that was required of them, she had to further prove that Slim 10 was the cause of the damages that she had suffered.

There could have been no direct evidence to show that Ms. De Cruz's liver failure was caused by Slim 10. Ms. De Cruz had to rely on experts' opinions and circumstantial evidence to show that Slim 10 was the highly probable cause of her liver failure. There were many expert witnesses who were called during the course of the trial to give evidence on whether it was Slim 10 that caused Ms. De Cruz's liver failure. The experts did not all share the same opinions but the court was convinced on all the circumstantial evidence that Slim 10 did cause Ms. De Cruz's liver failure in her case.

Personal liability of company's officers and shareholders

In this case, Ms. De Cruz's course of action against Semon Liu was based on the fact that he should be made personally liable because he authorised, directed and/or procured Health Biz's negligent acts. Semon Liu was the founder, director, president and principal shareholder of Health Biz.

The general principle in law is that the officers and shareholders of a company are separate and distinct from the company itself. Personal liability on company's officers and shareholders is generally not imposed except in exceptional circumstances. This is one of the benefits of limited liability afforded by a company.

On the particular facts of this case, the Court has found Semon Liu liable because his involvement in Health Biz was total. The Court was of the opinion that Health Biz by any other name would still be Semon Liu. Nothing in Health Biz was done without Semon Liu's knowledge or approval.

It was on these very exceptional circumstances of this case that Semon Liu was personally liable in negligence.

Damages awarded

Damages are allowed by the law to compensate a plaintiff in monetary terms for what the plaintiff has suffered and continues to suffer and not to punish the defendants. Punitive damages (i.e., damages for the purpose of punishment) are awarded only in very exceptional and limited cases.

Damages are claimable in tort by Ms. De Cruz only if the damage and the loss suffered by her were not too remote and were reasonably foreseeable.

Generally, there will be two kinds of damages which Ms. De Cruz can claim, namely special damages and general damages.

Special damages refer to the financial loss which Ms. De Cruz had already incurred in connection with her liver injury and transplant. These would include the medical fees and costs incurred for the liver transplant and her lost of earning as a result of hospitalisation.

Besides special damages, general damages are awarded to plaintiffs for the pain and suffering they had to go through. General damages refers to the non-pecuniary loss that Ms. De Cruz had suffered as a result of her liver failure. It is recognised that it is difficult to ascribe a money value that will commensurate with the loss that Ms. De Cruz have suffered. The Court will therefore adopt "conventional" figures which have been awarded for comparable injuries, making adjustments for inflation and the particular facts of the case. In deciding how much general damages Ms. De Cruz should be awarded, the Court had this to say:

"In awarding general damages, the court is attempting to compensate the injured party in monetary terms for what she has suffered and may continue to suffer. The plaintiff was hospitalized for 36 days between 16 April and 21 May 2002. She underwent a liver biopsy and then a transplant. She has also suffered from lethargy and jaundice, had hallucinations and vomiting. She also had to undergo numerous blood tests with the consequent taking of blood from her veins. Her physical activities and food preferences are now restricted. Although she has passed the first six months, the most crucial post-operation period, uneventfully, there is always going to be the nagging and gnawing thought whether the transplanted liver will fail or whether her weakened body will succumb to some disease or other. There will be risks to her and to the foetus if she should be pregnant. Visits to hospitals have become a way of life for this once vivacious young lady who is now uninsurable.

Is $250,000 too much compensation for this horrific list? Definitely not. I therefore award $250,000 in respect of this head of damages."

The Court also awarded damages for life-long medical costs that Ms. De Cruz will have to incur. The formula adopted by the Court in determining the quantum under this head of damages is: (Multiplicand) X (Multiplier). The multiplicand is the plaintiff's annual loss and expenses. The multiplier is the number of years by which to calculate the lump sum payment to be received by the plaintiff for future loss and expenses.

In Ms. De Cruz's case, the Court adopted that the average life expectancy for females in Singapore is 80. Ms. De Cruz was 29 years old at the time of the hearing. Taking this figure, the Court awarded a multiplier of 2/3 of the expected 51 years the plaintiff had to live (i.e., 34 years) bearing in mind the contingencies that may happen in life. This was one of the highest multipliers to be applied in Singapore.

Conclusion

Consumer protection is taken to yet another higher level with the decision in this case. It is comforting to know that vulnerable ultimate consumers of defective products do have legal recourses against irresponsible parties, even parties who sought to hide behind the veil of a corporate entity.

It would seem that consumer protection is developing in Singapore. Another welcome move in Singapore is the Consumer Protection (Fair Trading) Act which was passed on 11 November 2003. The Act, though passed, is not in force yet. When the Act comes into force in March 2004, it would be another victory for the consumers.

*Ms. De Cruz's case is now pending an appeal by the 3rd defendant, Semon Liu and the 4th defendants, TV Media. The appeal has been scheduled for hearing in May 2004.

Defective Goods
— Product Liability

Catherine Tay Swee Kian
Associate Professor
Department of Business Policy
NUS Business School
National University of Singapore
Barrister (United Kingdom); Advocate & Solicitor (Singapore)

Michael Low
Advocate & Solicitor
Sobhraj, Tay, Low, Subra & Teo

I. Introduction

X produces a dangerous defective product and sells to Y, who then re-sells to Z. Can Z sue X in tort (i.e., wrongful acts) for negligence?

Liability for defective products is essentially a mixture of a contractual and tortuous liability.

2. Contractual remedies

It would be more advantageous to a purchaser to claim in contract rather than in tort, if a contractual remedy is available. The reason is that the purchaser could rely on the implied terms as to quality and fitness for purpose of the goods under section 14(2) & (3) of the Sale of Goods Act, the Supply of Services Act, as well as the Unfair Contract Terms Act.

Privity of contract will deny any claim in contract to family members and friends or others, where their only remedy is in tort for negligence.

3. Manufacturer duty of care

The starting point for the tortuous duty of care in negligence is the landmark case of *Donoghue v Stevenson* [1932] AC 562. In this case, the plaintiff, Mrs. Donoghue, drank a bottle of ginger beer, bought for her by a friend and manufactured by the defendants. She became ill as a result of drinking the ginger beer, alleging that the bottle contained a decomposed snail. Mrs. Donoghue could not sue the retailer (she has no contract with, as she did not pay for the ginger beer as her friend paid for it). She sued the manufacturer of the drink for negligence. The court held that the manufacturer owed her a duty of care as she was an ultimate consumer.

Lord Macmillan said:

> "[The manufacturer] owes them a duty not to convert by his own carelessness an article which he issues to them as wholesome and innocent into an article which is dangerous to life and health."

Lord Atkin expressed the duty of care as:

> "A manufacturer of products which he sells in such a form as to show that he intends them to reach the ultimate consumer in the form in which they left him, with no reasonable possibility of intermediate examination, and with the knowledge that the absence of reasonable care in the preparation or putting up of the products will result in injury to the consumer's life or property, owes a duty to the consumer to take that reasonable care."

There could be liability for negligence under the famous "neighbour principle" as established by Lord Atkin:

> "You must take reasonable care to avoid acts or omissions which you can reasonably foresee would be likely to injure your neighbour. Who, then, in law is my neighbour? The answer seems to be — persons who are so closely and directly affected by my act that I ought reasonably to have them in contemplation as being so affected when I am directing my mind to the acts or omissions which are called in question."

The *Donoghue v Stevenson* case established that there could be liability in negligence for defective products. The test is reasonable foresight of harm to persons whom is foreseeable as likely to be harmed by one's own carelessness. "Products" can include any item capable of causing damage other than food or drink. The ultimate consumer is anyone foreseeably harmed by the defective product such as the user of the product including a bystander. Potential defendants can include a supplier of goods, a retailer or a wholesaler or a distributor[1], if circumstances are such as that he ought reasonably to have inspected or tested the products.

The mere opportunity that the product can be inspected after it left the hands of a manufacturer is no excuse. But the manufacturer's duty of care may be discharged if he has given a warning to test the product before its use[2].

4. Causation

Did the negligence cause the plaintiff consumer's damage? To establish negligence, a plaintiff consumer must prove that the defective product, e.g., a defective drug, caused the injury he is complaining of. Proving an increased risk of injury in drug induced harm will not by itself establish causation. One must infer a causal link to attribute the cause of harm.

In *Loveday v Renton* [1990] 1 Med LR 117, the plaintiffs could not prove that pertussis vaccine can cause brain damage in children, even though there is a possibility of a causal link.

There will be no liability for defective product if the plaintiff consumer is aware of the danger but ignored it. In

---

[1]See *Watson v Buckley, Osborne Garrett & Co.* [1940] 1 All ER 174.
[2]*Holmes v Ashford* [1950] 2 All ER 76, where manufacturer of a hair dye were held not liable when a hairdresser disobeying the manufacturer's instructions, and did not test the product before using on a customer.

such cases, the defendant's negligence did not cause the damage because of the intervening conduct of the plaintiff consumer breaking this chain of causation. However, knowing any danger will be useless, if the plaintiff could not avoid it anyway[3].

The defendant will not be liable if a consumer misuse a product in an unforeseeable way, as a manufacturer is liable only for damages arising from a product's contemplated use[4].

5. Duty to warn

An adequate warning from the manufacturer may discharge him of his duty of care. But the manufacturer may be negligent if there are no proper instructions for use from him. For example, a warning of a potentially harmful side-effects of a prescription drug is enough.

But there is no duty to warn of dangers that are obvious to the ultimate consumer[5]. If a danger ought to have been discovered, it is negligent to continue to produce the defective product and to do so without a warning. The manufacturer should in such cases take reasonable steps to recall the defective products or warn users of the dangers. A manufacturer's duty of care does not end when the goods are sold[6].

---

[3]See *Denny v Supplies & Transport Co. Ltd.* [1950] 2 KB 374.
[4]See *Aswan Engineering Establishment Co. v Lupdine Ltd.* [1987] 1 All ER 135.
[5]See *Deshane v Deere & Co.* [1993] 106 DLR (4th) 385. Also see *Nicholson v John Deere Ltd.* [1986] 34 DLR (4th) 542.
[6]See *Hobbs (Farms) Ltd. v Baxenden Chemical Co. Ltd.* [1992] 1 Lloyd's Rep 54.

6. Proving negligence

The plaintiff consumer has the burden to prove on a balance of probabilities that there is negligence. He must prove that the damage was caused by a defect in the product. It is recognised that where a defect arose in the manufacturing process, it can thus be difficult for a plaintiff to prove negligence[7].

Safety is of paramount importance here. Consumers expect food and drink to be not contaminated and that dangerous ingredients be labelled or warned. A warning, however, may make a defective product "safe".

The standard required is the reasonable care in all the circumstances. In certain products such as drugs, it may not be possible (and despite research) to predict all the risks of potential reactions for the whole community.

7. Losses

For a claim under negligence, where the defective products caused personal injury, the victim can claim for three types of losses. They are:

- Pecuniary losses are such as loss of earnings, medical expenses, travelling expenses and expenses for special equipment or caretaker. They are those capable of being calculated in monetary terms.

---

[7]See Michael A. Jones, *Textbook on Torts*.

- Non-pecuniary losses are those not calculable but will be awarded by the court on the principle of fairness and reasonableness. They include the compensation for the injury itself, pain and suffering and the loss of amenity. Loss of amenity refers to the loss of the use of that particular organ together with the loss of the enjoyment of certain activities.
- Future losses will be those like future medical expenses and care and future loss of earnings. The calculation for future loss of earnings is usually by multiplying the annual loss with the number of years of the loss. If the victim is not employed, e.g., a student, or employed at the same rate before the accident, the claim for future loss of earning will instead be a claim for loss of earning capacity, i.e., his capacity to find a equivalent job is reduced.

For all of the losses the injured victim is claiming, he has a duty to mitigate his loss. This means that he must try his reasonable best to shut the tap of his losses and not to allow the losses to flow incessantly.

Where the defective products caused death, the personal representative of the estate of the deceased shall be responsible for making the claim for negligence. Those claimable are:

- Pecuniary losses, e.g., expenses (including funeral expense) and lost of earnings.
- Non pecuniary losses, e.g., the injury, pain and suffering for period up to death only if the victim was conscious and lastly, loss of amenity regardless if the victim was killed instantly or never been conscious.

Additionally, the dependants of the deceased victim can make the claim for damages to compensate them for the loss of financial support that they had previously received from the deceased victim. Under this type of claim, there is an additional claim for bereavement.

For a claim under the contract, the buyer of the defective products can claim for damages. The damages will be any loss naturally arising from the breach and any loss which at the time of making the contract the seller could have predicted likely to result from the breach of it.

8. Who are responsible for product liability?

Persons who can be liable include:
- The producer/manufacturer.
- An importer.
- The supplier.

9. Defences available

The persons liable to the victim can rely on the fact of the victim's negligence in using the defective products. The victim may have failed to exercise reasonable care for himself and contributed to the negligence that caused the injuries or death to him. Such victim is said to be in contributory negligence. This is not a complete defence, but it helps to reduce the liability of the persons being sued with a corresponding result of the amount of the compensation being reduced.

The persons liable to the victim can rely on the fact that the victim has voluntarily agreed to assume the risk knowingly of its nature and extent and agreed not pursue the claim of the consequences. This defence is called *volenti non fit injuria*.

The persons liable can insert warning of danger in products. If the victim knew of the risk and assumed it, then *volenti non fit injuria* may be raised. If the victim knew of the risk but did not assume it and was negligence in using the products, then contributory negligence may be raised.

The persons liable cannot rely on contractual clause to exclude or limit their liability for negligence causing personal injury or death: Section 2(1) of the Unfair Contract Terms Act. For non-personal injury or death case, such contractual clause can be used subject to the test of being reasonable: Section 2(2) of the Act.

10. Limitation (under Limitation Act)

For personal injury and death cases, the victim must commence a suit in court within three years of his action accrued, simply meaning his entitlement to sue. The three years can also be from his knowledge of such entitlement, whichever is later. Beyond this period, the victim will be barred from suing.

For persons under disability at the time the action accrued, the three years run from the date when he is not under disability or death, whichever occurs first. There is no interpretation of disability under the Limitation Act; it is the author's view that disability refers to an infant or person of unsound mind.

For contractual claim, the limitation period is six years.

11. Ethics of misinformation and deception

Sales and contracts to sell are governed by the principle of *caveat emptor* — "Let the Buyer Beware" — which means it is the buyer's responsibility to determine the quality of goods purchased. Under *caveat emptor* the seller or producer need not inform the buyer about the defects in the goods sold.

However the seller must be truthful in his advertising or in packaging, and should not deceive or deliberately gives misinformation to the consumer which brings us to the ethics of withholding information. Deception or concealing information is harmful which can result in either physical, financial or social harm to others. This can be accompanied with trust being lessened in the deceiver.

12. Sale of Goods Act

Certain terms for the sale of goods are implied by the Sale of Goods Act so that the buyer receives benefits from the contract of sale.

Under Section 14(2) of Sale of Goods Act, there is an implied term that where the seller sells goods in the course of business, the goods supplied must be of satisfactory quality. But this term will not apply:

- If the buyer examines the goods for defects which such examination ought to reveal, before the sale contract is made; or

- Where the buyer is told of the defects before the contract is made.

Where the seller sells goods in the course of a business and the buyer makes known to the seller any particular purpose for which the goods are being bought, there is an implied term that the goods sold are reasonably fit for that purpose. But the buyer must rely on the seller's skill or judgment.

13. Misrepresentation

Statements are made in negotiations leading to a contract. A statement of fact which is untrue is a misrepresentation. Misrepresentation makes a contract voidable with the consumer, on discovering the misrepresentation, able to choose to rescind the contract of sale and treat it as if it had never existed.

A false statement is fraudulent if it is made knowingly or without belief in its truth or recklessly, careless about whether it be true or false. The misled consumer may sue for damages for tort of deceit. In fraudulent misrepresentation, the damages (i.e., monetary compensation) are calculated on tortious principles (i.e., putting the parties into the position before the wrongful act was committed). The misled consumer may rescind the contract with or without claiming damages for deceit.

Negligent misrepresentation is a statement made in the belief that it is true but without reasonable grounds for that belief. The misled consumer is entitled to damages for negligent misrepresentation as well as to rescind the contract of sale.

The Thin Line Between Consumers and Defective Products in Singapore:
Is it Time for
New Legislation?

Morris John
Advocate & Solicitor
Managing Director
Intellectual Property Law Department
Drew & Napier LLC

Stephen Norfor
Advocate & Solicitor
Associate
Drew & Napier LLC

I ntroduction

The statistics are out. About 23% of Singaporeans are obese[1]. But judging from the amount of excitement arising out of the recent Slim 10 case, it appears that there are a lot more Singaporeans who are not obese, but believe that

---

[1] See Yeo J. Obese? No short cut. 23 August 2003, Business Times Online Edition.

they are. For these people, it is probably no exaggeration to say that the concept of "thinness" has become more than just an overvalued idea; it has become an "overwhelming preoccupation"[2].

Yet who could blame them? Given our constant bombardment with images of perfect bodied people in every type of medium available, it is no wonder that many Singaporeans diligently strive to achieve that little bit of perfection in their lives. But as regular exercise regimes and healthy diets are notoriously difficult to maintain, many have turned to supposedly quicker-and-easier alternatives (such as slimming pills) to aid them in achieving such perfection. And with hundreds of inexpensive and celebrity-endorsed alternatives on the shelves nowadays, the temptation has never been greater.

But what happens when something goes wrong, as it did in the Slim 10 case? What can consumers do to ensure that those responsible for manufacturing and selling defective products compensate them adequately for their suffering?

Establishing a civil course of action

The traditional legal course of action has been one in contract. In this context, a consumer would generally be able to take legal action against a supplier of a defective product, on the grounds that such defectiveness constitutes a breach of the express or implied terms of the contract between them.

---

[2] See Fung D. Slim 10: Fat hopes? SMA News 34(7) July 2002.

However, a major problem with this traditional approach has been the requirement of a pre-existing contractual relationship between the parties involved.

To illustrate, where a consumer purchases a defective product directly from a manufacturer, he would be able to maintain an action against the manufacturer, as a contractual relationship exists between them:

The position would be different however, if the consumer purchased the defective product from a retailer; in such cases, the consumer's action would lie against the retailer, and not the manufacturer, as a contractual relationship would only exist between the consumer and the retailer:

Worse still, where a consumer did not purchase the defective product from either a retailer or a manufacturer (e.g., where he was given the defective product by a friend), the consumer would have no course of action against either the retailer or the manufacturer, as no contractual relationship exists between them.

To make up for these shortcomings, the law of torts has developed to provide consumers with an alternative course of action — one in negligence. In this context, a consumer would generally be able to take action against anyone in the supply chain of a defective product who possesses the required degree of fault (i.e., anyone who fails to exercise the due care that would be reasonably expected of him). This fault-based approach of determining liability provides the consumer with an important advantage over the traditional approach in contract: the ability to maintain an action against anyone in the supply chain, regardless of whether the consumer purchased the defective product from any one of them.

Nevertheless, pursuing an action in negligence against a manufacturer or distributor of defective products is seldom an easy task, as there are normally considerable evidential difficulties faced by a consumer in establishing the requisite degree of fault.

Furthermore, a manufacturer's or distributor's duty to exercise due care is limited, in the sense that it does not extend to cover unforeseeable risks or defects which are undiscoverable given the present state of technology. In the recent Slim 10 case, Health Biz Pte. Ltd. ("Health Biz") was held to be negligent for failing to keep proper records of pills that it had imported, and for failing to conduct proper batch tests (which could have revealed the presence of banned substances)[3]. But the result may have easily been different if

---

[3] See Popatlal A. Andrea De Cruz awarded almost S$900,000 in Slim 10 case. 4 October 2003, www.channelnewsasia.com.

Health Biz could have shown that it had followed the best practices available, and that the product itself had complied with all the guidelines and regulations laid down by the respective government authorities. In such cases, the consumer will almost invariably fail in his action, notwithstanding that the product was defective and resulted in the consumer suffering substantial injuries, or even death[4].

Strict liability statutory offences

Besides civil claims in contract and tort, criminal prosecution may also be available against a manufacturer or a distributor where a statutory offence has been committed. For example, Regulation 6 of the Medicines (Licensing, Standard Provisions and Fees) Regulations makes it an offence for a holder of a medicinal product licence to fail to comply with any of the standard provisions applicable to his licence[5]. Liability for such offences is often described as being strict, as it arises once the offence has been committed, regardless of whether the offender was at fault, or whether he had any contractual relationship with the victim.

In the recent Slim 10 case, as a result of the investigations conducted by the Health Sciences Authority, Health Biz was charged, *inter alia*, with eight counts of failing to comply with one of the

---

[4] This was what happened in the Thalidomide case. In the late 1960s, thousands of children were born with severe deformities due to the drug Thalidomide, which sought to help pregnant mothers reduce the effects of morning sickness.

[5] Another example can be found in Section 15 of the Sale of Food Act, which states that it is an offence to "sell any food which is unsound or unfit for human consumption".

standard provisions in its licence[6]. Due to the "irresponsible and haphazard" manner in which Health Biz managed the import of Slim 10, the maximum sentence was imposed on the company (i.e., $5,000 for each offence)[7], and its Import and Wholesale Dealer's Licence was revoked.

Criminal prosecution for defective products does not cost a consumer anything, and it is an effective mechanism for dealing with those who produce and sell defective products. However, from a consumer's point of view, a major shortcoming of criminal prosecution is that no compensation is provided for the injuries that a consumer has suffered.

Looking to the future

So what about the enactment of new product liability legislation in Singapore, in which strict civil liability is imposed on those in the supply chain of a defective product, and in which compensation is automatically provided for consumers who sustain injuries as a result of those defects? Arguably, this would be the best solution for consumers; it would offer the consumer a faster, less burdensome and more effective remedy against manufacturers and distributors of defective products.

---

[6] Namely, that it is not to sell or supply any medicinal product without a declaration that the product is free from poisons (e.g., fenfluramine) and any synthetic active substances.

[7] See Health Sciences Authority Press Release "Conviction of Health Biz Pte. Ltd. and revocation of its import and wholesale dealer's licenses" (26 September 2002).

Critics would argue that such a move would put manufacturers and distributors on the defensive, and that this would inevitably result in valuable products (e.g., anti-fat pills) being circulated years after their development, due to more extensive product testing. Some might even suggest that it would amount to the end of the health supplement industry, as the risk of liability to manufacturers and retailers would be unpredictable.

Nevertheless, a number of justifications for such strict liability can be advanced. As manufacturers and distributors benefit from the sales of their products, and create the risk of injury to consumers at the same time, it seems fair that they should be liable for any damages caused when a risk materialises. Furthermore, such liability for defective products can be offset by insurance, the premiums of which are distributable evenly amongst the consumers in the purchase price of the product[8].

But perhaps the greatest justification here is that strict liability for defective products goes a long way towards raising standards amongst manufacturers and distributors.

For all the above reasons, strict liability for defective products has already been adopted by a number of other jurisdictions:

a. United Kingdom / Australia

In the United Kingdom, the Consumer Protection Act 1987 was enacted to comply with the European Union's Directive on Liability for Defective Products 1985. Section 2(1) of the Act provides that

---

[8] The additional cost to manufacturers and retailers will not be unduly burdensome, as most already insure themselves against other types of liability.

where any damage is caused to any person by a defect in a product, the producer, importer and supplier (in certain circumstances) shall be liable for the damage. Such liability is strict; it arises once the product is deemed "defective", and there is no need to establish a duty of care on the part of either the producer, importer or the supplier, nor a pre-existing contractual relationship with them.

A strict liability regime was also introduced in Australia in 1992, by the insertion of Part VA into the Trade Practices Act 1974 (which was also based on the European Union's Directive on Liability for Defective Products 1985). In particular, Sections 75AD and 75AE enable any person who suffers damage from a defective product to recover compensation from the supplier of the defective product, without any need to establish negligence or breach of contract.

One perceived shortcoming of these Acts, however, has been the availability of a defence where a producer, importer or supplier can show that the defect was unknown and unforeseeable given the state of technology at the time when the product was put into circulation. This defence is commonly called the "development risks defence". Sounds familiar? Such a defence would also be effective in an action in negligence, as it would demonstrate the lack of fault on the part of the manufacturer or distributor. By expressly providing for such a defence, these Acts are open to the criticism that they are reverting to a fault-based approach in determining liability, and diluting the main advantage that a strict liability regime has over an action in negligence.

Notwithstanding this criticism, the UK Courts have adopted, to their credit, an extremely narrow view of the "development risks defence" in two recent cases:

i. In *Abouzaid v Mothercare*[9], a child suffered injury to his left eye whilst trying to attach a sleeping bag to his younger brother's pushchair. The injury was caused by a metal buckle attached to an elastic strap, which slipped out of the child's hands and lashed back. Mothercare raised the "development risks defence", arguing that it could not have foreseen the risk of this type of defect, as no such accident had occurred before. However, the UK Court of Appeal dismissed their defence, as the defect could have easily been discovered by performing a practical test (which Mothercare apparently had not thought of carrying out)[10].

ii. In *A v National Blood Authority*[11], a number of people were infected with Hepatitis C through blood transfusions. At the time of most of the transfusions, Hepatitis C had not been identified, and there was no test available to screen for the virus. However, it had been widely known in the medical profession, for at least a decade, that there was an unidentified agent causing post-transfusion hepatitis. The National Blood Authority raised the "development risks defence", arguing that the risk of infection was impossible to avoid, given the state of technology at the time of the transfusions. However, the UK Court dismissed their defence, and went on to hold that it became unavailable as soon as the risk of infection by the unidentified agent had become known.

---

[9] [2000] EWCA Civ 348.

[10] [2000] EWCA Civ 348, as per Chadwick LJ, at para 46.

[11] [2001] 3 All ER 289.

These cases make it clear that the "development risks defence" will only be effective to shield producers, importers and suppliers from liability in exceptional circumstances, such as where the defect is completely unknown and undiscoverable at the time when the product was put into circulation. In other words, the defence will not be an excuse for negligence (i.e., where the defect had not been discovered but could have easily been discovered), or recklessness (i.e., where the defect was known, but the product was still supplied because there was no way to identify which product had the defect)[12].

b. United States

As early as 1964, the American Law Institute drafted the 2nd Restatement of Torts, which attempted to extract the common law principles adopted by the US Courts at that time. Section 402A of the 2nd Restatement provides that anyone who sells a defective product which is unreasonably dangerous to a user or consumer, is subject to liability for the harm caused to the ultimate user or consumer, regardless of whether the seller has exercised all possible care in the preparation and sale of his product, or whether he has entered into any contractual relations with the user or consumer. Such liability is undoubtedly strict; liability depends not on the seller's fault or relationship with the consumer, but on whether the defective product is "unreasonably dangerous".

---

[12] The position under the Australian Trade Practices Act 1974 appears to be the opposite; see *Graham Barclay Oysters Pty. Ltd. v Ryan* [2000] 177 ALR 18.

Assessing the effectiveness of a strict liability regime based on Section 402A would require an in-depth analysis far beyond the scope of this article, especially given that it has neither been incorporated into state legislation, nor interpreted by the courts of each state, in any consistent manner. Suffice it is to say, though, that Section 402A has been incorporated, to some extent, in almost every US state, and that further developments in the law (such as the "defences" available to the seller) have been made on a piecemeal basis by the courts of each individual state, through the common law.

Although the American Law Institute has very recently incorporated many of these common law developments into a 3rd Restatement of Torts, thereby making some radical changes to the provisions of the 2nd Restatement, it remains to be seen how far the provisions of the 3rd Restatement will be adopted by statute and the common law.

But an excellent example of how the product liability regime adopted in the US can produce bizarre results is found in the case of *Uniroyal Goodrich Tire Co. v Martinez*[13]. In that case, *Goodrich* manufactured 16" tyres that came attached with a prominent warning label (containing yellow and red highlights and a picture of a man being thrown into the air by an exploding tyre) which clearly warned a user to:

i.   NEVER mount a 16" size diameter tyre on a 16.5" rim;
ii. ALWAYS use a tyre mounting machine with the hold-down device or safety cage or bolt to vehicle axle; and
iii. NEVER stand, lean or reach over the assembly during inflation.

---

[13] 977 SW 2d 328 (Texas 1998).

The plaintiff, an experienced mechanic, knew of these dangers, and even saw the warning label on the tyre. Nevertheless, he proceeded to mount a 16" tyre on a 16.5" rim (which he believed was a 16" rim), whilst leaning over the tyre assembly during inflation, without using a tyre mounting machine or bolting the tyre to the vehicle axle. The tyre exploded, injuring the plaintiff.

The plaintiff argued that the tyre was "unreasonably dangerous", as a safer alternative design for the product (i.e., a different tyre bead) could have reduced the risk of explosion. *Goodrich* claimed that the tyre was not defective as it bore clear and conspicuous warning labels, which if followed, would have rendered the tyre safe for use. They further claimed that it was the plaintiff's failure to heed the warnings which caused the accident.

The trial jury found that the tyre manufactured by *Goodrich* was indeed defective, and awarded the plaintiff an unbelievable US$17 million in damages. On appeal, the Texas Supreme Court upheld their findings, on the grounds, *inter alia*, that warnings were not a substitute for the provision of a reasonably safe design[14].

---

[14] The majority of the Supreme Court was clearly in favour of the adoption of Section 2(b) of the 3rd Restatement, which provides that a product is defective in design when risks could have been reduced by adoption of a reasonable alternative design, and the omission thereof renders the product not reasonably safe) over Comment J of the 2nd Restatement (which provides that where warnings or directions are given on a product for safe use, the seller is entitled to assume that they will be read and heeded, and thus, a product bearing such warnings or directions would not ordinarily be considered defective or unreasonably dangerous).

Arguably, strict liability regimes of this sort push consumer protection beyond the limits of common sense, and are open to the serious criticism that they subsidise the carelessness of a few consumers, at great expense to the rest who are more careful.

Conclusion

It is easy to conclude from the discussion above that the implementation of a product liability regime based on strict liability is never easy. In some ways, it appears to be a no-win situation: a more conservative approach (such as the one adopted in the United Kingdom and Australia) would be open to the criticism that it is does not do enough, whereas a more liberal approach (such as the one adopted in the United States) would be open to the criticism that it does too much.

Nevertheless, many countries have already been convinced of the justifications of strict liability, and have enacted at least some form of product liability legislation based upon it. Even China (the country from which the adulterated Slim 10 pills originated) has a Product Quality Law, of which Article 29 expressly provides that a producer shall be liable for compensation if his defective product causes damage to "human life"[15].

So perhaps it is time that we turned our minds to the question of whether we should implement our own brand of product liability

---

[15] They have adopted a conservative approach (i.e., the Article expressly provides for a defence where the "science and technology at the time the product was put in circulation was at a level incapable of detecting the defect").

legislation. At the very least, such legislation would make it easier for consumers who have suffered loss or injury caused by a defective product to claim compensation. But at its best, it might go a long way to prevent another Slim 10 episode from occurring again.

Arguably, a strict liability regime based on the UK approach would appear preferable, as it strikes a balance between all parties involved: on the one hand, it does not blindly punish manufacturers and distributors who are socially responsible; on the other hand, it befriends the consumer by reversing the burden of proof[16] and narrowly interpreting the extent of the defences available.

There is, indeed, a thin line between consumers and defective products in Singapore. And it is one which does not need any further slimming. On the contrary, it could do with a little fattening up. Let us hope, though, that it does not take another celebrity's misfortune to sell us the idea.

---

[16] It imposes on manufacturers and distributors the burden of proving why they should not be held liable, as opposed to imposing on consumers the burden of proving why the manufacturers and distributors should be held liable.

Consumer Protection and Product Liability
— The Statutory Framework

Steven Lam Kuet Keng
Litigation Partner
CS Lee
Notary Public
Commissioners for Oaths
Advocates and Solicitors

I ntroduction

The issue of product safety has recently been brought to lime light and has been the subject of much public scrutiny. Although traditionally the issue of whether a supplier, seller or manufacturer is liable to the buyer or user for a defective product is determined by the use of contractual or tortuous principles, one must also bear in mind that Parliament has provided for statutory liabilities in these circumstances as well. The primary legislation for the governing of this area is the Consumer Protection (Trade Description

And Safety Requirements) Act (Cap 53), which is worded similarly to the English Trade Descriptions Act 1968.

Essentially, the preamble to the Act states that this is:

> "An Act to make provisions prohibiting misdescriptions of the goods supplied in the course of trade; to confer power to prescribe requirements relating to informative marking and advertisement of goods and to their safe composition, construction or design, and for purposes connected therewith."

Other more specific Acts governing the supply of medicines and drugs are the Medicines Act (Cap 176) and the Poisons Act (Cap 234).

Statutory framework for general product liability

Strict liability

Basically, Section 4 of the Consumer Protection (Trade Description And Safety Requirements) Act (Cap 53) states:

> "Subject to the provisions of this Act, any person who in the course of a trade or business:
> (a) applies a false trade description to any goods; or
> (b) supplies any goods to which a false trade description is applied, shall be guilty of an offence."

And it is further stated in Sections 5 and 6 that:

"**5.** For the purposes of this Part —

(a) a false trade description means a trade description which by reason of anything contained therein or omitted therefrom is false or likely to mislead in a material respect as regards the goods to which it is applied or in connection with which it is used, and includes every alteration of a trade description whether by way of addition, effacement or otherwise which makes the description false or likely to mislead in a material respect; and

(b) a false indication, or anything likely to be taken as an indication which would be false, that any goods comply with a standard specified or recognised by any person or implied by the approval of any person shall be deemed to be a false trade description, if there is no such person or no standard as specified, recognised or implied.

6. (1) A person applies a trade description to goods if he —

(a) affixes or annexes it to or in any manner marks it on or incorporates it with —

(i) the goods themselves; or

(ii) anything in, on or with which the goods are supplied;

(b) places the goods in, on or with anything which the trade description has been affixed or annexed to, marked on or incorporated with, or places any such thing with the goods; or

(c) uses the trade description in any manner likely to be taken as referring to the goods.

(2) An oral statement may amount to the use of a trade description.

(3) Where goods are supplied in pursuance of a request in which a trade description is used and the circumstances are such as to make it reasonable to infer that the goods are supplied as goods corresponding to that description, the person supplying the goods shall be deemed to have applied that trade description to the goods."

As there is no mention of *mens rea* or any mental element in Section 5, the offence is treated as one of strict liability tempered by statutory defenses, and as such the mere fact that the offender had no intention to commit the offence is of little relevance, if not no relevance to the issue of guilt, but may have an impact as a mitigating factor for the issue of sentencing[1].

Any person?

In respect of the term "any person", although normally it would deal with the actual seller of the goods, one must note that the English cases suggest that liability could be imposed even if the person applying the false trade descriptions is the buyer of the product[2] and even if he is not a contracting party to the transaction[3] (such as when he makes a false remark about

---

[1] *Sweet v Parsley* [1970] AC 132.

[2] *Fletcher v Budgen* [1974] 2 All ER 1243.

[3] *Fletcher v Sledmore* [1973] RTR 371.

the product which he is selling to someone, who buys the product from him and who subsequently resells the product to a third party who has heard the false remark made by him).

As such, if for example a computer retailer is to tell one of his private customers that the latter's personal computer which is not working properly is only of scrap value and then goes on to purchase the same from the customer for a nominal sum of say $1 and does minor reformatting which would cost no more than $50 and goes on to sell the same as a reconditioned computer say for $800, it may be a case that false trade description may have been applied by the computer retailer.

As the Act is targeted at people who are acting in the course of business and trade, the transaction must be of a commercial nature and liability would not extend to parties who are not acing in a commercial or business relationship. Thus, if the sale of the product is not the ordinary business of the seller, he may not be liable under the Act[4]. However, one must also bear in mind that even two to three transactions over a couple of months may be construed by the courts as ample sufficiency for a trade pattern to be established under the Act[5].

Apply?

The word "apply" has also been given a wide interpretation to include oral statements[6]. However, one must note that the English cases

---

[4] *Davies v Sumner* [1984] 3 All ER 831.

[5] *Devlin v Hall* [1990] 155 JP 20.

[6] Section 6(2).

seem to suggest that post-contractual statements would not come under the ambit of the Act[7] as these statements are not connected with the sales of the product. Thus it would seem that there is a requirement of some form of reliance by the buyer of the false statement made and the statement must be associated in some way or another with the sale or supply of the goods[8]. The false description must also be connected with the goods supplied and not with the services relating to the goods for liability to be attached[9].

False trade description?

What then is a false trade description? Basically, the purchaser need not be deceived by the statement made by the seller and the offence would be committed if the description is technically true but is still misleading or it is false to a material degree[10].

However if only statements of opinions or mere-puffs are uttered, they would not amount to false trade descriptions. Thus if one says that one's product is of "extra-value", it may be construed as only a mere-puff and would thus not amount to a false description[11]. However if the statement could relate to a feature of the product, such as by saying a second-hand

---

[7] *Wickens Motors (Gloucester) Ltd. v Hall* [1972] 1 WLR 1418.

[8] *Formula One Autocentres Ltd. v Birmingham City Council* [1999] RTR 195.

[9] *Wycombe Marsh Garage Ltd. v Fowler* [1972] 3 All ER 506.

[10] Section 5(a).

[11] *Cadbury v Halliday* [1975] 2 All ER 262.

car is a "beautiful" car that could be construed as meaning that it is roadworthy, then a false description may have been applied[12].

On this point, it must also be noted that the packaging of the goods could amount to the trade description being applied. Thus in a case where the face cream was contained in a bottle with a false base, even though the bottle correctly states the amount of the contents, it was held that a false trade description had been applied[13]. Thus even if the trade description is technically true but de facto unable to perform up to the specifications alleged, then an offence would be committed. As such in the case of *Dixons v Barnett*[14], where the specifications for a telescope was stated as capable of 480 times of magnification whereas only 120 times was the effective magnification, the court found that the seller to be liable for applying trade description.

Goods covered?

It is interesting to note at this juncture that in the English case of *Stainthorpe v Bailey*[15], and even free gifts could be the subject matter of a false trade description.

Furthermore, under Sections 7 and 8 covers the situations of advertisements and trademarks containing trade descriptions and they state:

---

[12] *Robertson v Dicicco* [1972] RTR 431.

[13] *R v A and F Pears* (Times, 27th October 1981).

[14] (Guardian, 14th June 1988).

[15] [1979] Crim LR 677.

"7. (1) This section shall have effect where in an advertisement a trade description is used in relation to any class of goods.

(2) The trade description shall be taken as referring to all goods of the class, whether or not in existence at the time the advertisement is published —

(a) for the purpose of determining whether an offence has been committed under Section 4 (a); and

(b) where goods of the class are supplied by a person publishing or displaying the advertisement, also for the purpose of determining whether an offence has been committed under Section 4 (b).

(3) In determining for the purposes of this section whether any goods are of a class to which a trade description used in an advertisement relates, regard shall be had not only to the form and content of the advertisement but also to the time, place, manner and frequency of its publication and all other matters making it likely or unlikely that a person to whom the goods are supplied would think of the goods as belonging to the class in relation to which the trade description is used in the advertisement.

8. A trade description which is or is part of a trade mark within the meaning of the Trade Marks Act

1998 may be a false trade description when applied to any goods, except where all of the following conditions are satisfied:

(a) it could have been lawfully applied to the goods if this Act had not been passed;

(b) on the commencement of this Act the trade mark either is registered under the Trade Marks Act 1998 or is in use to indicate a connection in the course of trade between those goods and the proprietor of the trade mark;

(c) the trade mark as applied is used to indicate such a connection between the goods and the proprietor of the trade mark or a registered user of the trade mark under the Trade Marks Act 1998; and

(d) the person who is the proprietor of the trade mark is the same person as, or a successor in title of, the proprietor on 1st August 1975"

Furthermore, Section 14 deals with false representation as to supply or approval of goods and which states:

"**14.** (1) If any person in the course of any trade or business gives by whatever means any false indication direct or indirect that any goods supplied by him or any methods adopted by him are or are of a kind supplied to or approved by any person including any government or government department or agency or any international body or agency whether in Singapore or abroad, he shall, subject to the provisions of this Act, be guilty of an offence.

(2) Subsection (1) shall have effect without prejudice to any written law prohibiting or restricting the use of any name, emblem, insignia, seal, flag, pennant, title, coat of arms, sign, words or letters or any other form of description…"

Thus it is clear that the extent and breadth of the Act is quite wide.

Disclaimers

What about the use of disclaimers to limit liability? It is enlightening to note that in the case of *Norman v Bennett*[16], the court noted that in order for the disclaimers to be effective, the disclaimers must be "bold, precise and compelling, and must be effectively brought to the notice of any person to whom the goods may be supplied".

The intention is to protect innocent traders who may not be fully aware of the nature of the products and goods supplied to them by third parties. Thus in the case that it is the supplier who applied the false trade description, then the use of disclaimers would not absolve them of liability[17].

---

[16] [1974] 1 WLR 1229.

[17] *R v Southwood* [1987] 3 All ER 556.

Penalty?

Basically, under Section 15 the penalty that may be imposed by a court is a fine of not exceeding $10,000 or to imprisonment for a term not exceeding two years or both.

Personal liability of corporate officers

Where a company commits the offence, the directors and other senior officers would be personally liable if they had consented and had connivance to the commission of the offence or the offence is attributable to any negligence on their part[18].

Defences

On the point of the defences available to the supplier, basically a due diligence defence is provided under Section 19 that states:

> "**19.** —(1) In any proceedings for an offence under this Act, it shall, subject to Subsection (2), be a defence for the person charged to prove —
> (a) that the commission of the offence was due to a mistake on his part or to reliance on information supplied to him or to the act or default of another person, an accident or some other cause beyond his control; and

---

[18] Section 17.

(b) that he took all reasonable precautions and exercised all due diligence to avoid the commission of such an offence by himself or any person under his control.

(2) If in any case the defence provided by Subsection (1) involves the allegation that the commission of the offence was due to the act or default of another person or to reliance on information supplied by another person, the person charged shall not, without leave of the court, be entitled to rely on that defence unless, within a period ending seven clear days before the hearing, he has served on the prosecutor a notice in writing giving such information as was then in his possession identifying or assisting in the identification of that other person.

(3) In any proceedings for an offence under this Act of supplying goods to which a false trade description is applied, it shall be a defence for the person charged to prove that he did not know, and could not with reasonable diligence have ascertained, that the goods did not conform to the description or that the description had been applied to the goods..."

Basically a defence is afforded to the supplier if he took all reasonable precautions and exercised all due diligence to prevent the commission of the offence.

The English position on the due diligence defence suggests that there may be a loop-hole, in that if the offence is committed by a store employee and the company seemingly has a system in place to prevent the application of such trade descriptions then the company may not necessary be liable[19]. However, it is submitted that a court hearing the matter is likely to and should take into consideration that a corporation has in place to ensure compliance to determine whether due diligence had been carried out accordingly.

Innocent supply of goods

Furthermore, if the supplier is just an innocent supplier who relied in good faith the good reputation of his supplier, he may be afforded a defence under Section 20, which states:

> "20. In proceedings for an offence under this Act committed by the publication of an advertisement, it shall be a defence for the person charged to prove that he is a person whose business it is to publish or arrange for the publication of advertisements and that he received the advertisement for publication in the ordinary course of business and did not know and had no reason to suspect that its publication would amount to an offence under this Act."

However for this defence to be available, the supplier must still take some effort to verify the information provided to him by his own

---

[19] *Tesco v Nattrass* [1972] AC 153.

supplier. It is submitted that this is good as it ensures that the well-being of the consumers would be at all times be on the mind of the suppliers[20].

Effect of a conviction for the breach of the statutory regulation

The impact of a conviction of a supplier under the statutory provisions is that it is likely to have an adverse bearing against him in his subsequent defence of any civil proceedings taken against him. It must however be noted that in the event of a conviction, it does not necessary mean that the claimant's case is indefeasible. In reality the supplier could argue a case of contributory negligence on the part of the claimant (depending on the facts of the case), arguing that the claimant has not taken reasonable care of his own well-being[21]. However, it is humbly submitted that the conviction would feature heavily on any reasonable person's mind in the civil trial of the matter.

---

[20] *Barker v Hargreaves* [1981] RTR 197.
[21] *Geetha v Hong Kong Teakwood Works Pte. Ltd.* [1992] 1 SLR 920.

Behavioural/Ethical
Perspective

Advertisements for Slimming Products:
A Behavioural Perspective

Audrey Chia
Associate Professor
Department of Management & Organisation
NUS Business School
National University of Singapore

S ocial science research has revealed that people's judgements and decisions are not always rational. For instance, judgements are influenced by psychological framing. If I try to sell a certain brand of sunscreen by emphasising the good effects of wearing a sunscreen (protecting skin from sun damage, looking younger), I would probably be less successful than another person who sells the same sunscreen but presents the same facts using a "loss" frame (not wearing sunscreen leads to skin damage and premature ageing). This is because, according to Prospect theory (Tversky and Kahneman, 1981), people are more sensitive to losses than gains and therefore would generally be more risk-taking in a "loss" frame than in a "gain" frame. Where there is a potential for loss, an individual's motivation to reduce his potential loss of magnitude X would be higher than his motivation to make a gain of X in another situation where there is a similar potential for gain.

Research on human reasoning in the area of behavioural decision theory and decision-making has shown that people use heuristics when making decisions and judgements. Although efficient, these heuristics sometimes lead to less than rational judgements.

Researchers have exploited such knowledge in the area of asset management (see http://www.fullerthaler.com/). The main phenomena that such investment strategies take advantage of are overconfidence on the part of most investors and anchoring (failure to adjust one's judgement and position sufficiently in the face of new data). Much of the research on application of social science findings on human reasoning and judgement has focused on financial decisions such as when to enter the stock market and which stocks to buy. These applications rest on assumptions about investor behaviour, for example, that most investors will, for example, be slow to dump poorly performing stocks from their portfolios (anchoring to initial beliefs about how good the stock is and failing to adjust their positions even when there is information that the stock will not meet expectations). Asset managers such as Fuller and Thaler take advantage of this slowness to adjust and dump the poor performers before most other investors do and the price plunges. An illustration of the application of behavioural finance, entitled "The Madness of Crowds" was reported in a recent issue of *Forbes* magazine (27 October 2003).

We may also extend the application of research on behavioural judgement and decisions to the context of advertising. Knowing that people's judgements are influenced by framing, that people commit fallacies in reasoning and that people use heuristics when making decisions, advertisers can create advertisements that capitalise on consumers' cognitive habits and weaknesses.

There is one important difference between the application of behavioural research in marketing and financial contexts. In the financial applications there are no attempt to influence the investment decisions of investors in general. Behavioral decision theory is used more to predict how investors will act, and asset managers then decide how to act on the basis of those predictions. However, in marketing applications, there is an attempt to influence people before the buying decision is made. These applications are found in a variety of advertisements but for the purposes of this article, I shall focus on those that promote beauty and slimming products and programmes. A major ethical problem with these applications is their strategic exploitation of people's cognitive habits (Singer, Singer, Lysonski and Hayes, 1991).

Exploiting the reliance on heuristics

Because of the time and cost needed to understand information, people rely on heuristics to make even important decisions that involve money and life. For instance, it may be too difficult and time-consuming to weigh all the pros and cons of the various forms of slimming treatments, so consumers' decisions may simply be guided by heuristics and logical short-cuts. Among these is the availability heuristic, in which information that is more vividly presented, readily available or recent is given greater weight in decisions and judgements than other less vivid, less readily available or less recent information.

Advertisements that exploit people's tendency to use the availability heuristic tend to feature vivid "before" and "after" pictures of people who have successfully slimmed down, among them are well known public personalities, television stars or models. These pictures are usually the focus of the advertisement. The vivid, pictorial information provided in these advertisements is likely to be given more weight in the average consumer's mind and have more influence on the consumer's decision than the fine print that states that "results vary from individual to individual" because it is presented in lively detail and takes up most of the advertising space.

Logical fallacies

Slimming advertisements may also exploit people's susceptibility to logical fallacies. A logical fallacy commonly found in slimming advertisements is *post hoc ergo propter hoc*, in which an event that follows another is thought to be the consequence of the first event. Many advertisements for slimming programmes present cases of women who lost weight after taking part in the slimming programme after delivering their children. However, regardless of whether they enrol in slimming programmes or not, women do lose weight after childbirth. There may be other reasons for weight loss, for instance, breastfeeding, increased activity and lower food intake but in the advertisements all the weight loss was attributed to the slimming programme. A more reasonable comparison would pit the average postpartum weight loss against the average postpartum weight loss of all women who had undergone the slimming programme.

Other logical fallacies that may be present in slimming advertisements are:

- The false dilemma: either go through this slimming or beauty programme or be ugly, unwell and have low self-esteem;
- Appeal to irrelevant authority, usually, the words of an attractive spokesperson who may know little about the technical aspects of the slimming or beauty products;
- Hasty generalisation from the examples of a few successful cases of slimming/beauty enhancement; and
- Unrepresentative sample: the results achieved by the women shown in slimming advertisements may not be representative of the results of the particular programme or product. However, people may form conclusions about the efficacy of a slimming programme or inflate their hopes for slimming down after viewing the unrepresentative sample of stunning cases presented in the advertisements.

Setting standards for comparison

Many slimming advertisements present stunning cases of success. While it is reasonable for slimming companies to report their very best success stories, the practice of doing so also presents unrealistic models for comparison. Viewers may be well aware that these cases are not average, but the repeated presentation of these success stories may exert framing effects. The cases may change a viewer's reference point by shifting her into a "loss" frame. In simple terms, a woman who may have originally felt quite comfortable with her own weight of 55 kg may shift her point of reference when she reads about other women shedding weight from say, 58 to 50 kg. So while she may have been quite neutral about being 55 kg, she may shift into a "loss" frame when a weight of less than 55 kg is repeatedly presented as the standard. The shift probably has emotional effects, such as dissatisfaction, but more important, it has cognitive effects on decision-making. A loss frame makes one more willing to take risks and probably more willing to try slimming products.

Questionable presuppositions and normative pressures

We may analyse slimming advertisements in terms of the values or presuppositions embedded in them. Slimming advertisements often contain one or more of the following presuppositions:

- Slimness and beauty are inextricably linked.
- Slimness is tied to self-esteem; one cannot feel confident if one is not slim.
- Slimness is the foundation for well-being, vitality and health.

When we examine the presuppositions, however, we may find that none of them is logically or empirically true. The first presupposition, for instance, adopts a superficial, physical definition of beauty. Regarding the second, we have to question why people who are not slim may feel less confident. Is it because of the crushing pressure from advertisements in the first place? I discuss this further in the next paragraph. Moreover, there are other ways to enhance confidence such as learning to speak better and impoving one's knowledge or skills. The third presupposition is also faulty because health depends on other factors like nutrition, rest and so on. The ethical problem here is that these presuppositions are not just flawed but also repeated across advertisements for different slimming products and programmes. These repeated messages from the presuppositions may mislead consumers and lead to poorer quality of decision-making.

Cumulative effects

Another related concern with slimming advertisements stems from the images of beauty that these advertisements promote. A similar concern was raised in the context of fashion advertisements. Bishop (2000) argued that in themselves, individual advertisements that portray unrealistic standards of beauty (e.g., airbrushed, poreless complexions) may not pose ethical problems. However, taken in total, such advertisements constantly and cumulatively emphasise the overwhelming importance of the physical aspects of self and impose standards that are unrealistic for most of the population. The same can be said of slimming advertisements that can be found daily in newspapers and other "in-your face" advertisements that pop out from web pages, pharmacy doors, television and magazines. Collectively, the advertisements communicate and reinforce the slim body type as the ideal, and reject other body types as unacceptable. Together, they promote an overly narrow definition of beauty and wellness and in effect, a lopsided view of the self and its worth. While it may be interesting or entertaining to view such advertisements, their cumulative effect may be to harm some viewers' self-esteem and mislead them into ignoring the social, spiritual and other aspects of self.

References

Bishop JD. Is self-identity image advertising ethical? *Business Ethics Quarterly* **10**(2):371–398. 2000.

Singer AE, Lysonski S, Singer M and Hayes D. Ethical myopia: The case of framing" by framing. *Journal of Business Ethics* **10**:29–36. 1991.

The madness of crowds. *Forbes*, 27 October 2003.

Tversky A and Kahneman D. The framing of decisions and the psychology of choice. *Science* **211**:453–458. 1981.

Are There Shortcuts?

Sebastian Anthony
Head
Institute of Management and
Allied Health Sciences
National Healthcare Group (NHG) College

Introduction

Reading the newspaper everyday brings one to many advertisements on weight loss or weight reduction. Many promise that there are no exercise routines, no strict diets, no pain, no pills, etc. Is that really true?

In our fast paced lifestyle where we are used to fast and efficient service in hotels, shopping centres, supermarkets, restaurants, and many other necessities in life, we also expect the same when it comes to ourselves. If you really think about it, is that really unreasonable? We are fast

and efficient at work, we are highly competent in what we do and we are able to produce work that has a high standard in terms of quality and we are able to produce it in double quick time. So why cannot we expect the same from our physical self?

The law of the harvest

I had the opportunity to visit Europe once, where I came across many farms. While talking to some people who used to work on these farms, it made me realise that how difficult the life of a farmer was.

Early in the season, he had to work hard to till the soil and time was spent planting the seeds. More time was spent tending to the young plants, ensuring that they did not get too much or too little of sunlight, water and nutrients. Then there was the danger of pests and the always, uncertain weather. Finally came harvest time.

Consider a situation where no tilling was done followed by no seeds being planted. How much of harvest could the farmer bring in at the end?

A famous quotation by Samuel Smiles comes to mind, "Sow a though, reap an action; Sow an action, reap a habit; Sow a habit, reap a character; Sow a character, reap a destiny."

The battle of the bulge has to begin with a thought or a vision.

The power of visioning

Stephen Covey in his book, *7 Habits of Highly Effective People*, mentions, "Mental creation precedes physical creation." Would an architect start building a building or structure without a blueprint? Yet, many start "building" their bodies without having a clear picture of the final product.

You may be tempted to ask and answer this very pertinent question, "How would I look when I lose 15 kilograms?" Please do not. Ask instead this of yourself, "How do I see myself when I am 70 years old?" If you are able to picture yourself living up to the ripe young age of 70, then I hardly think that you would picture yourself looking fat and sloppy. I imagine, that you would want to look not a day older than 50 even though you are 70, you would also be fit, having a good time with your grandchildren, family and friends. You would even have a very busy and physically demanding schedule as you go about working, contributing to the community and having a game of golf or tennis at the club. Lofty dream or possible reality?

Firstly, get out of the short-term mentality of just losing weight. Short-term objectives of losing weight or taking a few inches off the waist will get you into trouble faster than not wanting to lose weight at all. Have you ever wondered why those extra pounds always return when the dieting stops or when the pills run out?

Short-term results do not usually last because there has not been any real work done in creating a new habit.

Vision statement

Begin first by creating a vision statement for yourself. Having a vision alone is not enough. It has to be backed up by a powerful, inspirational and moving statement.

Many organisations have a vision statement that helps to inspire and motivate their staff members. Having a vision in mind is not enough; it has to be written down so that you can refer to it every single day.

Here is an example of a vision statement by Thomas Jefferson, which may hold lots of truths for us all.

Decalogue

1. Never put off till tomorrow what you can do today.
2. Never trouble another for what you can do yourself.
3. Never spend your money before you have it.
4. Never buy what you do not want, because it is cheap; it will be dear to you.
5. Pride costs us more than hunger, thirst or cold.
6. We have never repented of having eaten too little.
7. Forget the mistakes of the past and press on to the greater achievements of the future.
8. Wear a cheerful countenance at all times and give every living creature you meet a smile.
9. Give so much time to the improvement of yourself that you have no time to criticise others.

10. Be too large for worry, too noble for anger, too strong for fear, and too happy to permit troubles.

— Thomas Jefferson

If you had a chance to change the decalogue above, how would you use it to suit yourself?

Perhaps, it might go this way;

1. Never put off exercising till tomorrow, when you can do it today.
2. Never cause another to swim or run on your behalf.
3. Never spend your money buying exercise machines that never get used.
4. Never buy snacks or tit-bits, because they were cheap; it will be dear to you.
5. Pride not to acknowledge the overweight, flabby self costs us more hunger, thirst or in our case the humidity.
6. We will repent from having more than necessary.
7. Forget the failed diets of the past and press on to the greater healthy achievements of the coming future.
8. Wear a cheerful countenance, even when dieting and give every living creature a smile.
9. Give so much time to the improvement of your physical, emotional, mental and spiritual growth that you have no time to gossip about the physical appearance of others.
10. Be too large for self-pity, too noble for anger at yourself, too strong for fear of getting started, and too happy to let past failures get you down.

Getting started

Having a great vision statement is fine, but if it is just stays there, it is quite useless. How many times have you encountered a situation where you were served by a rather indifferent or even rude sales or counter staff, only to find the mission and vision statement hanging on the wall just behind the sales or counter staff?

The vision must be translated in action, but how?

Any success in life requires three key components, aptly named Key Success Factors (KSF), they are, *Know-how, Intensity* and *Practise.*

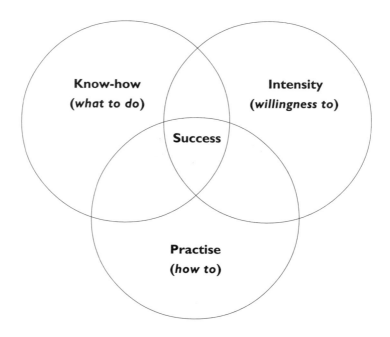

Know-how

The *Know-how*, is the aspect of tacit knowledge of the subject. In this case, it is the knowledge of losing weight. Gaining knowledge about weight loss is really not very difficult. We can begin by doing one or more of the following:

- *Seeking medical advice*: It is always advisable to seek medical advice from your family doctor or a physician who has a good background of your medical condition. He would then be able to advice you on the types of exercises or dietary control that you may need to observe in your quest in losing weight.
- *Joining a gym:* You may want to consider joining a recognised gym or scheduled exercise routine headed by a qualified gym instructor or trainer. Again, the gym instructor or exercise therapist or trainer may be able to advice you on the various kinds of exercise routines that may suit you depending on your weight, physical attributes, goals that you intend to achieve for yourself as well as likes and dislikes.
- *Seeking advice from a dietician:* Similar to seeking medical advice, you may want to consider consulting a qualified dietician. A dietician will be able to help you in the selection of various kinds of foods for daily consumption that will give you the required levels of energy to sustain your required activities for the day. Over a period of time, you would eventually begin to lose weight, thereby achieving your desire goal. It would be ideal to make and keep regular appointments both with your dietician and doctor.

- *A combination:* This is always a sound method, in which, you first seek medical advice, then going on to meet with your dietician and exercise therapist or trainer and review your success with all of them.

Intensity

The aspect of motivating oneself to accomplish the set goals or objective is the *Intensity*. It comes from deep within and it is the engine that drives the individual towards the end result.

How many resolutions did you make at the start of the year? How many of them did you accomplish at the end? Why do you think that many people start off very strongly in wanting to keep these resolutions only to give them up after only three weeks into January. The answer is obvious and simple, the lack of desire or intensity.

So the question is, "How does one develop and keep the desire?".

You may have encountered a situation when you were out on vacation for a couple of weeks and upon your return trying to start your car. You hear the engine crank up but it just refuses to start. Similarly, we too will find any new task difficult to do for the first time. As Newton argued, "A body at rest, will tend to stay at rest". So here are some pointers on how to keep the *Intensity*:

- Make an appointment with your doctor, dietician or trainer and block off the time in your planner or PDA.

- If dieting, write out your diet plan and display it at your work space or home so that it is clearly visible to you.
- If exercising, write out your exercise routine on a weekly basis and block off the time in your planner or PDA (do not change it for anything).
- It always helps if you exercise with a friend or members of your family.
- Read your mission statement on a daily basis.

Practise

Having the *Know-how*, coupled with the *Intensity* is only two legs of a three-legged stool. The final leg of the stool is the *Practise*, for without which there will be no success.

Nike says, "Just do it", and it is precisely that. No excuses, no compromises, just practicing integrity and courage to accomplish the goal set, that is, to lose weight.

Even if friends or family members who promised to go jogging with you do not show up, or your boss just gave you a last minute assignment or you were asked to have a business lunch with an important client, remember integrity and courage.

The integrity to stay true to yourself and the goal that you set coupled with the courage to politely but firmly turn down, switch with a colleague or to look at alternative arrangements for last minute work assignments or personal commitments that are not aligned to what you are seeking in terms of losing weight.

Of the three KSF listed above, perhaps the most difficult to confront is *Practise*. The first two are rather theoretical or cognitive exercises while *Practise* is very action oriented.

Conclusion

We began this chapter by asking you to imagine when you are 70 years old, thereby moving away from the short-term mentality. By sticking to the three KSF mentioned here and constantly practising integrity and courage at the moment of choice, you will eventually form a habit that will guarantee that your weight problem will never come back. However, it does not mean that you cannot indulge yourself once a while but you are also disciplined enough that once a while does not become a daily event.

Appendices
to the Slim 10
Episode

| Compiled by
Editorial Team, World Scientific

R efer to Appendix 1 and 2 for reports on the investigations of the ingredients contained in Slim 10 by Singapore's Health Sciences Authority. Appendix 3 focuses on some issues surrounding the regulations of slimming products.

Appendix 1
Health Sciences Authority reports
on Slim 10 investigation

On 4 June 2002, the Health Sciences Authority (HSA) issued a report of the Slim 10

investigation. The following are the main points of the press release:

1. From end March to early April 2002, the HSA received four adverse drug reaction reports that were suspected to be associated with Slim 10 consumption. Two reports were of symptoms of hyperthyroidism, one report was of irregular menstruation and one report was a case of hepatitis. HSA responded by taking samples of Slim 10 from the market for testing.

2. Analysis of the samples revealed the presence of nicotinamide, also known as Vitamin B3, in significant amount but not at levels associated with toxicity. As this was an undeclared ingredient in Slim 10, HSA decided to withdraw the product from the market as the presence of nicotinamide cast doubts on the integrity of the product. On 15 April 2002, HSA instructed the importer of Slim 10, Health Biz Pte Ltd, to fully withdraw stocks of Slim 10 from the market by 19 April 2002.

3. HSA also issued an alert to healthcare professionals on 15 April 2002, informing them to look out for any adverse reactions associated with Slim 10 and requesting them to report any such reactions to HSA.

4. On 29 April 2002, HSA confirmed the presence of Fenfluramine, a synthetic pharmaceutical agent for the treatment of obesity controlled under the Poisons Act. On 30 April 2002, the HSA advised the public to stop taking the product with immediate effect and to destroy their remaining stocks or surrender them to HSA.

Appendix 2
HSA updates on Slim 10 adulteration

On 18 June 2002, the HSA issued an update of the Slim 10 investigation. The following are the main points of the press release:

1. The HSA has detected an additional adulterant in Slim 10 — thyroid gland components, the active principles of which are substances controlled under the Poisons Act. Slim 10, a Chinese proprietary medicine (CPM), has been withdrawn from the market since 19 April 2002 after the presence of nicotinamide was detected. Subsequent testing revealed that Slim 10 was also adulterated with a slimming drug, fenfluramine, which had been withdrawn from the market since 1997.

2. Health Biz and its president and director Semon Liu have been charged with eight counts of contravention of Section 5 of the Poisons Act with respect to the adulteration of Slim 10 with fenfluramine.

3. The presence of thyroid gland components in Slim 10 was confirmed by HSA on 14 June 2002. The detection and confirmation of the presence of this biological substance involves a very complex analytical process using specific enzymes to yield the active principles, thyroxine and triiodothyronine. These substances produce the effects of thyroid hormones in the body and lead to signs and symptoms of hyperthyroidism when consumed.

4. This finding of thyroid gland components in Slim 10 explains the symptoms of hyperthyroidism in the adverse drug reaction reports from healthcare professional to HSA. Symptoms of

hyperthyroidism include weight loss, headache, anxiety, nervousness, rapid heart beat, palpitations, tremors, intolerance to heat, sweating, increased pulse and blood pressure, menstrual irregularities, abdominal cramps and frequent bowel movements (usually diarrhoea).

5. These effects are transient and should subside 1–2 months upon discontinuation of exposure to the thyroid hormones. There should be no long-term adverse effects on those who have experienced these symptoms.

6. Health Biz and Semon Liu are issued a further eight counts of sanction each for contravening Section 5 of the Poisons Act by selling Slim 10 containing the active principles of thyroid gland, substances controlled under the Poisons Act, without a Poisons licence.

7. They have also each been charged respectively for failing to keep import records, as required by Standard Provision 5 (1) in the Second Schedule to the Medicines (Licensing, Standard Provisions and Fees) Regulations. A proper import record is essential for monitoring and tracking the import of medicinal products and their compliance to requirements.

Appendix 3
Regulation of the importation and sale of slimming products

1. Synthetic medicines, commonly known as Western medicines

- Synthetic pharmaceuticals for treatment of obesity are regulated as Prescription-Only Medicines in Singapore. Such medicines are used in the short-term treatment of obese individuals in conjunction with an overall weight-loss programme under medical supervision. Where consumers are considering self-medication with other products that claim to cause weight loss, they have to be cautious and discerning and exercise care in the selection and use of these products.
- All synthetic medicines are stringently evaluated by HSA for their quality, safety and efficacy before marketing approval is granted.
- After marketing approval has been granted, these products are subjected to post-marketing surveillance that includes quality compliance testing and Adverse Drug Reaction monitoring.

2. For other products promoted as being useful for weight reduction, ranging from Chinese proprietary medicines (CPM) and health supplements to other complementary or traditional medicines, their claims cannot be evaluated by HSA since rigorous scientific data to validate efficacy and benefits are generally not available. Instead, such products are regulated on the basis of safety and quality of the product.

Chinese Proprietary Medicines

- Generally considered to be relatively less toxic, because they usually comprise herbs in low individual concentrations and, in the case of traditional medicines, because of long historical usage.

- Licensing of CPM dealers — importers, wholesalers, manufacturers and re-packers, to ensure accountability for the safety and quality of their products.
- Pre-market product assessment to ensure that products are from licensed manufacturers, sold freely in country of origin, do not contain Western medicines or naturally occurring toxic substances, and that heavy toxic metals, such as mercury, arsenic, lead and copper, and microbial counts are within permissible limits.
- Submission of test reports and written declaration of the absence of any synthetic drugs or poisons as defined in the Poisons Act by the licensed importers for every consignment imported.
- Approved product labelling in English to clearly specify the ingredients, indications for use, dosages, batch number, expiry date and the identity of the importers and manufacturers.
- Where there is any doubt on the documents submitted by the applicants, product samples are tested by HSA's laboratories to exclude suspected adulterants, and analyse toxic heavy metals and microbial contents.

Health supplements and other traditional remedies like Jamu and Ayurvedic preparations

- There are currently no licensing requirements for their import, manufacture and sale, but dealers are required to ensure that the products do not contain any prohibited substances and the toxic heavy metal content does not exceed legally permissible limits.

Slimming treatments, such as the use of equipment for slimming, the use of slimming oil and body wraps, etc.

- Not regulated

3. HSA carries out regular post-marketing surveillance and runs a quality-testing programme on products sold in the market to ensure compliance with legal requirements.

4. HSA has an Adverse Drug Reaction (ADR) Monitoring System to detect any adverse reactions of products used in Singapore, and this is tied to international ADR networks to pick up early signals and intelligence on any problems with health products. Health care professionals are requested to report suspected adverse drug reactions encountered to HSA so that unsafe products can be removed from the market as and when they surface.

5. A question surrounding the regulations issue is: why Slim 10 was allowed to be sold for five months before any action was taken by HSA?
   - Anybody who wants to import a CPM submits an application to HSA and tells HSA what the product contains. HSA will test the product and make sure that the product is as declared. On that basis, HSA will allow it in.
   - On every consignment, the importer will then have to declare that the consignment of the product coming in does not have any of the items in the Poisons Act, does not have any heavy metals or any microbial contents above the legal limits.
   - In the case of Slim 10, considered a Chinese medicine, the importer declared the ingredients in the pill, HSA tested that

they were indeed there but it was not possible to test what else was not there.

- The issue was debated in the Singapore Parliament on 20 May 2002. Below are quotes from Lim Hng Kiang, then Health Minister:

"Let me give another analogy. When I was in charge of the Ministry of National Development and we imported vegetables from Malaysia and we had this problem of pesticide residue. We could impose a very strict regime because the number of known pesticides used is limited and we can test for the 10 or 15 pesticides and make sure that the residue does not exceed the level that we set. Therefore, we can have a very tough system in testing every consignment for those 10 or 15 pesticides and make sure that it does not exceed the residue level.

"But when we come to Chinese medicine, we do not have a similar list of things we can say that you cannot put these in the Chinese medicine. We can have a list of the poisons, but they will be put in steroids and all kinds of stuff, and they may put in things which are above the safe dosage. So it will be very difficult for us to do tests on every consignment and to test for what is not declared as ingredients in Chinese medicine. That is why in 1999, when we were looking at how to regulate Chinese medicine, we decided that it is not possible for the HSA to license every product and every consignment. Therefore, we put the responsibility on the importer, the wholesaler, to make sure that whatever they bring in they must declare that the product they bring in does not have the items in the Poisons Act, do not have heavy metals, and the ingredients of the product are clearly labelled."

"[H]ealth products cover a wide range and when it relates to pharmaceutical products, the so-called Western medicine, because these are synthetic, and chemicals, they pose higher risks. The HSA's stand is to regulate this stringently.

"At the other end of the spectrum, when it is Chinese medicine, because these are herbs and plants, and these are traditional medicine which have been in use for hundreds of years and proven to be reasonably safe, we have to take a different approach. Unfortunately, the problem now is that many people bring in Chinese medicine but actually they adulterate it with Western medicine, and they come in under the guise of pure Chinese medicine. This is the middle area that we have to review and make sure that even though we cannot regulate the efficacy, we must regulate for safety, and that is the intention that we set out."

Sources:

Appendix 1: http://app.internet.gov.sg/data/hsa/PRelease_4 Jun 02_HSA %20Reports%20on%20Slim%2010%20Investigation%20&%20Enforcement %20Action_HSA%20website.doc

Appendix 2: http://www.hsa.gov.sg/docs/PRelease_HSAUpdatesOnSlim10_18 Jun 02-HSA %20website.pdf

Appendix 3: http://www.parliament.gov.sg/Publication/Htdocs/H2005.htm

Social/Community
Perspective

Case Studies of
Anorexic and
Bulimic Patients

Chou Mei Ling
Psychologist
Deputy CEO
Carecorner Singapore

C ase 1: Over dieting

Elsa, a gaunt 15 year-old, was brought to the counselling centre by her concerned mother. The parent was worried that if the girl were to go on refusing to eat anything, she would die. Standing at 158 cm and tipping the scale at 34 kg, Elsa's skin was dark and looked like she was suffering from poor blood circulation. Her blouse and tight skirt were loose and blowing in the wind. I remembered vividly that she, a frail girl with an angry facial expression, sat defiantly in the meeting room and refused to follow us into the counselling room. She maintained that she was normal and did not need any counselling.

Elsa's elder sister told me that had it not been the nutrients and appetisers that their mother secretly put into Elsa's drinks, Elsa would have died of hunger. The sister also revealed that when Elsa was in Secondary One, Elsa was unhappy that her classmates called her names like "Fatty". She demanded that her mother stop giving her "food that will make her fat". But the mother felt that Elsa was not fat, had no need to diet at all and insisted that Elsa finished her rice. Elsa could not go against the mother openly, so she resorted to pouring away the food when her mother was not looking.

Elsa's figure was thinning by the day, but she still felt that she was overweight. In contrast, the mother felt that Elsa was overly thin and tried ways and means to make her eat. At the same time, Elsa's father was having an extra-marital affair and wanted to divorce her mother. The mother then directed her anger and disappointment towards the father into forcing Elsa to eat more. As a result, the mother and daughter relationship suffered as they fought with each other over the issue of eating.

After the divorce proceedings were settled, Elsa felt very sad. She begun to eat even less and her body shrunk drastically to stick-like. Later Elsa was hospitalised after she fainted from malnutrition. Under the care of doctors and nurses, Elsa's weight managed to climb back to around 34 kg. The mother was very worried that Elsa would be hospitalised again, maybe even lose her life.

Counsellor's analysis

Teenagers like Elsa are very sensitive of their self-image and in particular their body image. Bodily changes during puberty are frequently subjected to criticism and comparison among peers, and every teenager wants to be accepted or praised by his or her friends. So, when Elsa was called "little Fatty" by her classmates and it might just be a harmless tease, it actually made her determined to go on a diet.

If the mother had lent a listening ear to Elsa and shared her own growing up experience, it would have given some support and points of reference to Elsa. Maybe then Elsa would not have taken her classmates' words too seriously. If mother and daughter had gone on to discuss about ideal body weight and reach a consensus to carry out that plan, this would have been a valuable chance to forge a more intimate parent-child relationship.

But it was a pity that the lack of communication between mother and daughter led them to shut each other out. The added stress of a broken family caused Elsa more frustration and confusion. This would have been a simple issue of dieting, but the additional psychological factor escalated the problem to anorexia nervosa. A vicious cycle built over the long term almost cost the life of the girl.

Anorexia nervosa is a person's protest against the loss of control over his/her own life. Sufferers do not know how to express their needs, and also could not find other ways to satisfy their needs. They feel they could not control themselves, their relationships with others and almost every other aspects of life. To stop eating seems to be the only thing they can do, and it becomes the only means to escape from the conflicts and pressures of life.

Anorexia nervosa can cost lives. If its signs are detected and treated early enough, lives could be saved. Sufferers of anorexia nervosa show one or more of the following symptoms:

- More than 15% under the ideal body weight.
- Not overweight, but insist on dieting.
- Overly thin, but insist on being too fat.
- Worry endlessly about food, calorie, nutrition and cooking.
- Denial of hunger.
- Over exercising.
- Eating small meals but complaining of bloatedness.
- Excessive checking of one's weight.
- Loss of body hair.
- Feeling cold, even if surrounding temperature is normal or slightly low.
- Irregular periods.

When too much of dieting graduates into anorexia nervosa, the patient needs professional help. Treatments can include psychological therapy (such as about oneself and family), nutrition therapy and drug therapy. Therapies that can help the patient to express his/her feelings, such as art, dance, exercise and drama, are also conducive.

Case 2: Can't stop eating

Mei Fong, 26 years old, was dragged to the counselling centre by her friends. She was in constant depression because of boy-girl relationships and had attempted to commit suicide on several occasions. After being dumped by her long-term boyfriend two years ago, Mei Fong was constantly in and out of relationships in a spiteful manner. Whenever she was in a depressed mood because of another breakup, she would keep on calling her friends and eat non-stop until she needed to throw up all the food she had consumed. After a round of eating and vomiting, she would repeat the cycle again.

Mei Fong used to be an air stewardess with a pretty face and a shapely body. But she became quite fat, weighing more than 80 kg with a height of 160 cm. Her cheeks were bloated, eye bags were fluffy and she had double chin. She looked old for her age. Her hands and legs were as big as an elephant's! The only features that still looked pretty were the lush eyelashes and prominent double eyelids.

Whenever Mei Fong was feeling down, she would gobble up all the food in the house. Her family and friends tried to hide the food, but she always managed to find them. Her family members finally had to stop buying any food back. If there was nothing to eat, she would drink and even take drugs. After being sacked by her company, she had been staying at home for more than two years and was living off her boyfriends and family members.

Mei Fong wanted to pull herself together to slim down, but she could not control her craving for food. She also could not shore up the energy to exercise. Her solution? Go for a $6000 treatment at one of the commercial slimming centres. After one or two sessions, she realised that she could not pay for the treatment charged to her credit card. Already, her other payments had been overdue by a few months, and it would be disastrous to add this huge sum of $6000! Mei Fong even asked me if the counselling centre could help her pay! She knew she had entered into a contract with the slimming centre and could not back out of it. She was afraid of debtors going after her! I was really worried to see her landing herself in hot soup!

Counsellor's analysis

Mei Fong is a classical case of bulimia. This is a condition whereby a patient develops an abnormal intake of food while trying to escape the conflicts and pressures of life. In contrast to anorexia nervosa, sufferers eat non-stop to calm their mood swings. This condition is usually accompanied by messy relationships, over-spending, drug and alcohol addiction, over-exercise, etc. Patients also feel that they have lost control over their lives, just as sufferers of anorexia nervosa do.

The biggest tell-tale sign of this condition is that whenever there is a mood swing, the patient consumes food uncontrollably and then throws up. His weight fluctuates greatly. He feels guilty or shameful about eating and thus forces himself to vomit after a meal. For Mei Fong, she tried very hard to control her food intake but was not successful at all. In the long-term, sufferers may develop cryptorrhea, unbalanced chemical secretion, disruption of menstruation periods, damage to the teeth, chest and kidney, depressive moods, lethargy, etc. Extreme cases may even result in death.

Mei Fong sometimes displays the symptoms of compulsive overeating. Its sufferers consume a large amount of food until they feel very uncomfortable. However, this condition is not life threatening, as sufferers do not develop the habit of throwing up after eating. The side effects include high cholesterol, diabetes, heart problems, depression, etc. Patients often eat until they are very bloated, but they could still make themselves stop eating if they want.

In order to help Mei Fong, we need the cooperation of a psychologist, a psychiatrist and a nutritionist. An intensive therapy would be better suited to control the illness. The therapy could include how to manage self-respect, drug and alcohol addiction, sense of loss, sexual hurt, survival after trauma, family structures, body image, inter-personal relationship, self affirmation, nutrition, eating patterns, etc.

One point to note is that people who develop problems linked to abnormal intake of food are mostly women (though recently there are male sufferers too). Therefore ladies, please take heed, think carefully of what you really want, or otherwise you could be caught in a trap unknowingly!

Size Matters:
The Smaller, The Better

Aditee Ghate
Executive Committee Member 2003
AWARE (Association of Women for Action
& Research)
Communication and Facilitation Specialist
Adhem Enterprises

Over the last two years, Singapore's healthcare industry has been in the news — for reasons other than SARS.

Count among these the controversial Hormone Replacement Therapy (HRT), which, according to recent US studies, resulted in severe side effects to women dealing with menopausal issues and created confusion among the regular users.

The other big issue has been slimming — and the things that women do to reduce body fat and weight (such as the infamous Slim 10 episode).

The almost fatal incident of a local television actress and the actual death of another local woman — both of whom consumed Slim 10 — have highlighted the dangers of these pills.

Yet, even now, the newspapers and media are full of ads exhorting the miraculous results of slimming salons, body toning sessions, dieting and slimming pills. Have we not all seen those embarrassing — nay, appalling — ads where a woman triumphantly talks about the happy changes in her married life because she lost the weight she gained after childbirth? And those ads about the woman's pride at having "saved" her marriage — by going back to her "original size" after childbirth.

Does it not make you wonder what values are being espoused here? And the underlying message being sent to mothers? That the hormones which help the woman's body to blossom in readiness for motherhood are just not acceptable for her husband — in his eyes she has become "less" of a woman by having a "more" womanly body.

Is there a consciousness that the mantle of "superwoman" now places yet another onerous burden on Eve: being slim, always.

And this is a "requirement" that has been identified by society, for centuries on end. All this, in spite of the reality that there are three billion women in the world and only a handful of them are models whose "figures" would fit the definition.

Let us understand why.

What, really, is beauty?

Beauty has meant different things in different centuries. And the one thing that has not changed throughout history is that the definition of beauty has been imposed on women.

In Victorian times, a woman was considered a beauty based on the size of her waist. If a man's palms could span her waist, the woman could consider herself the ultimate beauty.

Did you know that, in those days, women who wore girdles suffered fractured ribs and displaced spleens? And these injuries, or, "sacrifices" as society preferred to call them, were considered acceptable for women!

Take another example, somewhat closer to home. In ancient China, the size of the woman's feet was considered a sign of beauty. The "highly desirable" achievement of "lotus feet" (which involved binding the feet so that they remained the size of a little child's feet), permanently crippled thousands of hapless young girls — leaving them unable to walk without support.

Today, this cruelty has just taken a different disguise: beauty is now defined by the slimness of a woman's body.

Just look around. Are we not all obsessed by the need to be slender?

How many women do you know work out or walk into slimming salons or take slimming pills because they are concerned about their health? And how many do all this to make themselves acceptable to society?

And let us not even touch upon the extreme ways a woman is ready to reduce her fat: operations, liposuction, the stapling of the stomach lining and many depressing others.

SLIM Chance   FAT Hope

Most women know that slimming pills have life threatening side effects. And they know that visits to the slimming salons do not help to maintain weight (or the right curves) once the treatment is over.

Yet, they do not stop.

What is it that drives a woman to push herself to such extremes to look slim? What does she think she gets in return? Why is she so obsessed with her looks and her slimness?

Could it be because being slender is the sign of power, of being in control of their lives, of being "beautiful"?

Movies like "Shallow Hal" touch on these issues beautifully. Even though it was a comedy, the underlying message could not be ignored. In a pre-release interview, the leading lady, Gwyneth Paltrow, admitted that she became aware of the judgements society makes on a fat woman in the course of the film's shooting.

During one of her evening shoots, she took a break and visited one of her regular bars in the full gear of the "fat" woman in the movie. What unnerved and astonished her was the treatment she got. People did not recognise her and, therefore, everyone in the bar, including the bartender, ignored her because they only saw a really fat woman. And when she ordered her drink, the bartender would not even meet her eyes. It was, she said, like she did not exist!

For all her physically imposing presence (courtesy of her fat woman costume), Gwyneth said she felt non-existent in that bar that night. It was a sobering moment for her to realise the extent to which the "fat" woman becomes an object in the eyes of society. She is no longer a person.

The reality is that you are considered a success if you are slim and slender. Any woman who is plump or big-boned is considered a failure in society. To put it bluntly, she is made to feel like she has failed society.

More is more, so is less

For a deeper understanding of this, just look at what the feminist movement of the 1970s paralleled with: the age of eating disorders. We all know, today, that a majority of those struck by eating disorders are women. Do we wonder why?

> Kim Chernin, in her book *Womansize: The Tyranny of Slenderness*, outlines the dilemma faced by women. She writes (I am quoting her verbatim here) about the implications of the two parallel movements — the feminist movement on the one hand, and the self-help (weight-watching) group of women who suffer from eating disorders.
>
> The feminist group meets to explore ways and means to empower women. The self-help group on the other hand meets to control their bodies.
>
> Listen to the spontaneous metaphor, she writes, that finds its way into the discussions of these two groups.
>
> In the feminist group it is *largeness* in a woman that is sought, the *power* and *abundance* of the feminine, the assertion of a woman's right to be taken seriously, to *acquire weight*, to *widen* her *frame* of reference, to be *expansive*, *enlarge* her views, *acquire gravity*, *fill out* and gain a sense of self-esteem.

It is always a question of *widening, enlarging, developing* and *growing.*

In the weight-watching groups though, the women are trying to *reduce* themselves; and the metaphoric consistency of this is significant: they are trying to make themselves *smaller,* to *narrow* themselves, to become *lightweight,* to lose *gravity,* to be-*little* themselves.

Here, emphasis is placed upon *shrinking* and *diminution, confinement* and *contraction,* a *loss* of pounds, a *losing* of flesh, a *falling* of weight, a *lessening.*

The book helps us to see that the woman who chooses to lose weight is doing so because she seeks approval from society — to be accepted, to be loved and to be popular. A woman's success today is also defined by how "good" she looks, i.e., the slimness of her body.

The size of a woman should be a very subjective individual preference. Human beings are meant to come in different sizes and shapes.

During teenage (and especially after childbirth) a woman's body blossoms. It takes on a curvaceous rounded form that identifies her gender. A woman is intended to have full thighs, rounded hips and breasts, and curved arms. Ironically, it is in these very stages of her life that women are afflicted by eating disorders.

The reason? A woman's "desirable" dimensions are still determined by society.

What is it that society is so afraid of — that compels it to diminish the woman in some way for her to be an acceptable part of society?

More importantly, what compels a woman to accept these standards? Why does she sacrifice something, make herself small in one way, less in others. Why does she desire to have a body that is not intended for her?

Damned if she does, doomed if she doesn't

A woman's identity over the years has been dependent on the various roles she has played. A mother, a daughter, a wife, a daughter-in-law, and, in recent times, a professional.

With more and more women working their way up the corporate ladder, the "homemaker" (the new, politically correct term for housewives) is considered to be a step below the professional woman. A woman with a profession, on the other hand, married and having children, is considered the ultimate woman.

The modern woman takes on the mantle of the perfect wife, the ideal mother and the dynamic professional without batting an eyelid. She feels liberated by the opportunities that life has offered her. She genuinely believes that this lifestyle represents "equality".

Interestingly, nobody notices, least of all women, that despite all the dramatic progress women have made in the male bastion, there has been none made by men in the female bastion.

What makes women believe they are truly free when they are bearing more responsibilities today than they ever did in the history of humankind? Is this what the women of the 1970s sought when they came onto the streets seeking equality? Is this what they were working towards?

We do not have a noteworthy percentage of men taking care of households or children to warrant any statistics that would suggest a trend.

It is no wonder that the few, rare men who venture into the woman's domain are still making headline news. A man choosing to let go of his career to take care of his home and children is considered exceptional news. The same way that women in the 1960s or 1970s were given attention for stepping out of the traditional roles society had imposed on them.

Today, the woman who manages the house and the career, the superwoman, is passé. There is nothing exceptional about what she achieves. She herself does not want to consider it as anything other than the given... what she ought to do.

But it seems like even though she has conquered this, it is not enough!

Now society has added one more trial: her slimness, for having had the audacity to walk into what is even today a dominantly male world.

Are women doomed to live their lives based on what is expected from them by society? Who makes these rules?

It's still a man's world

The patriarchal society we live in may allow some power to the woman but not without extracting a pound of flesh. When a woman joins the workforce and becomes an executive, she is expected to live by the rules of the man's world. Ergo, she is expected to be non-emotional, objective, pragmatic and realistic when she lives in this world.

Is this how we would really describe the psyche of a woman?

Yet, a lot of women have successfully managed this. They are known to be power-hungry, driven, workaholics, tough and hard as nails — and these are women who proudly claim that being a "woman" has not made any difference in their rise up the corporate ladder.

A woman is expected to model the mindset of a man in his world. There is no space for her to be herself, to be different from men and still live in their world. The reality is that society has neither changed its infrastructure nor its systems or values to fit the difference of having a woman in the corporate world.

Women are either in or they are out. They either play by the rules laid down by men or they do not play at all.

And when women follow these rules — by being assertive, knowing their minds, being ambitious, and letting the family take a back seat — they are seen as "unfeminine".

Another example of what women have given up to be equal to men is the dialogue you hear at bars and restaurants where young women openly share their sexual exploits.

We have come a long way in being able to make choices about our sexual relationship without being labeled. At the same time, I wonder to what extent we are playing by the rules of the man's world.

Is it not obvious that young men today and for centuries have been having a similar dialogue about their sexual exploits? So what value have we added to our acceptance as women, our individuality, and our existence by relishing that we too can play by the rules of a masculine culture?

What does a woman make of these contradictory messages?

Why women fear independence

Let us look at the differing ways in which men and women or boys and girls are brought up by the same set of parents.

Studies have shown that girls are handled less energetically than boys. Even though we are aware that girls are sturdier and mature faster than boys, they are seen as more fragile.

Most girls are expected to sit politely and watch their brothers (even younger ones too) indulge in overtly and excessively physical activities, e.g., climbing trees. The mother worries about her daughter falling off a tree and hurting herself — there is no such fear about the son.

Mothers believe they are "protecting" their daughters by not letting them run wild, while their sons' enthusiasm to climb trees is seen as being "manly".

There is evidence that boys are weaned away from dependency at as young an age as two years, while girls remain protected until they are six years old, and even during teenage.

The message sent to a two-year old boy crying is that mommy is not going to rush to make things ok because he needs to learn how to be a "man". A two-year old girl, on the other hand, knows, from very early on, that mommy is definitely going to come to help.

It has also been found that parents have perceived the crying of a baby as "fear" when it is a girl and as "anger" when it is a boy. Which is why parents rush to assuage the girl's fear, while allowing the boy to be angry — he can just vent his anger and then be alright.

These preconceived notions of the differing abilities of boys and girls result in the latter growing up to believe that they are expected to be dependent on others for help. That they would not be perceived as feminine if they expressed too much independence.

At the same time, we have the modern superwoman — who strives to conquer more and more of the world, by taking on responsibilities that no human being can take on and live to tell the tale.

With these wildly contradictory messages, what do you expect from women? Clarity? Identity? Sanity?

In his book *The Genealogy Of Morals*, Friedrich W. Nietzsche, the late-19th century German philosopher, reflects on the need to critically scrutinise the ideals we live by — and the need to change them as times change.

He asks, "Would anyone care to learn something about the way in which ideals are manufactured? Does anyone have the nerve?"

Do you?

Being Fat Can be Beautiful Too!
— Interview with Moses Lim

Interviewed by
Editorial Team, World Scientific

1. What do you think of your body shape? Does it bother you?

It depends on how you approach it. If I were in a business that emphasises on beauty, then it would be a problem. But if I were in the food business, it would not be an issue at all. I am on the large side since eight years old until today; I have forgotten how it is like to be thin! So, you have found the right person to speak on the topic!

Having come all this way, I realise that being fat is not a problem, nor is it a sin. Oprah

Winfrey once had a programme on being fat and she had the same sentiment. So, I think the focus should actually be on how you got fat. Everybody has his or her own life story and learning journey until the day he/she leaves this world. Each day we learn and sometimes, we make mistake. Children tend to like certain kinds of food and then suffer indigestion because of overeating. For adults, we are also greedy and eat too much of some stuff. But the difference is, adults can control themselves. If we do not have enough exercise and eat too much, then of course we will become fat. It can be too late when you finally discover that you are overweight.

Would you believe me if I tell you that for all these years, the idea of slimming down has never crossed my mind? Of course I wanted to diet and slim down, but after years of experimenting with different ways and means, I have only one conclusion which I often relate to my friends who are also fat. That is, if you think you cannot solve the problem of being too fat, then why not focus on making yourself healthy? This is my stand as a fat person. My point is, health should come before outward appearance. You can go ahead to try to change your body shape, but if you still fail in the end, why not spend all the time and effort on working on your health instead?

I have been seeing my family doctor regularly every month, for almost 30 years. You can opt instead to go for a yearly medical checkup, but should at least do some exercises on a regular basis. Since three months ago, I have been attending gym sessions twice or three times weekly. I exercised for an hour each time, working on the different machines. This is what I meant by working on health rather than on appearance.

It is not necessary that fat people have a lot of illnesses, skinny people can be quite problematic too.

2. Can you share with us your experiences in dieting? Have you ever used slimming pills before?

I have tried all kind of ways. I have taken some pills before, but my doctors prescribed them. I personally feel that drugs are only effective if you are just starting to get fat, as the weight gain is not steady yet. But not for someone like me, whose body shape is almost permanently fixed. Even if I lose 5 kilograms of fats, you would not be able to see it. But if you want me to reduce my weight by 30 kilograms, that would be quite a big deal! So, I might as well concentrate on improving my health. If I am healthy, the fats would also go away. My health would go some way to compensate for the fatness.

3. Has any slimming centre or product approached you to be its spokesperson?

The funny thing is, nobody has approached me before! I have always joked that whoever dares to hire me as its spokesperson, that company will become very famous. But if nobody has approached me, it makes me wonder if their products are really effective! You see, I am the most obvious person to endorse for their products, and the fact that nobody wants me, means that there is a big question mark on the effectiveness of the products! But I am not so thick-skinned to ask them if they want my service! This seems to have cemented my observation that these products might only be effective for someone who has just started to become overweight.

I used to head a group called "The Fatty Club", and all the members want to slim down. Once, they tried to follow the "protein diet", that is, by only eating meat and no vegetables or tomato sauce. I tried it too and lost about two to three kilograms. But this is very unhealthy! If you want to diet, you have to do it in a healthy way. If you can slim down and still maintain good health, episodes like the Slim 10 affair would not have happened!

4. Do you find that your body shape has helped you in your career?

Well, you cannot really say that it has helped me in my career. The reason may be that when I entered the entertainment line, there was nobody like me, so I became famous for my body shape. Just think about it, during the era when I first became a child actor, it was quite difficult to find someone of my size. That time, most children were skinny and it was quite a curiosity to see a fat kid, so audiences found me to be cute! It is very different nowadays, where there are so many over-sized children. It has to do with the change in times.

Our lifestyle has changed over the years too. There were no such things as instant noodles, Styrofoam lunch boxes, and coffee dispensing machine, etc, during my time. These are all chemically treated stuff, yet modern people are using more and more of them. Therefore, being fat does not necessarily mean you have eaten too much, there may be other reasons. We need to view fatness from a broader perspective.

5. If one day you were to slim down, do you think it will affect your acting career?

Then I will accept it as part and parcel of life, and the fact is, I am trying hard to slim down. I feel I have come to a stage where the change will not affect my career. To put it simply, I will not become as skinny as Wang Sha (the thin half of 1960s comedy duo Wang Sha and Ye Feng), as there is a limit to how much weight I can shed. Furthermore, Singapore is so small and everybody in the entertainment circle knows me and accepts me as who I am. So there is not much difference if I am fat or thin. On the other hand, if I am a newcomer fresh from the Star Search competition and suddenly have a drastic change in body shape, then maybe people will start talking. Perhaps there will be some people who prefer the old me, but that is not going to affect my career at all. I have come such a long way that I do not care whether it affects me or not.

6. Some actors have concentrated on being comedians to gain a foothold in the entertainment line. Are you afraid of being stereotyped?

I am not afraid of being stereotyped. If you define "stereotype" from the perspective of body shape, then I am already limited by my size.

But if you mean it as typecast to be a comedian, then I can tell you that it does not bother me at all. At this stage of my career, I am able to choose and pick what I want to do. Like in the drama series, "Always on My Mind", which was about SARS, I was totally different from the past and acted as a vegetable seller who was a very proud person.

There are many ways of projecting myself in a comedian role. I act differently in "Under One Roof" and "Comedy Night". In the former, the comedy is closer to life and is aimed at promoting family values. As for the sketches in "Comedy Night", they tend to be exaggerated and over-the-top, just for the laughter. I am able to choose whether I want to be part of a particular show, not just blindly following what others want me to do. Directors also know that I like the challenge of doing new things. I once acted in a community movie where I was cast as a stroke sufferer. This was an entirely different experience for me, as I had to speak with a crooked mouth. This goes to show that, if you are confident of yourself, you can always try out new roles.

7. If somebody challenge you to shed a certain amount of weight for the sake of a role, what would your reaction be?

Actually, two to three years ago, we had a concept for a TV programme that required audiences to guess how much weight I would lose the next week. We were at the initial stage of conceptualising the show, but eventually it did not materialise.

To me, it was a big challenge. As it was going to be a game show and a reality show at the same time, I'd really have to go about losing my weight. But was I up to it? There were only six days before the next episode, maybe I could not shed half a kilogram, or maybe I could lose up to two kilograms? I could not be sure, the audiences could not be sure too, and this would be the draw of the show. Although it was a bold concept, I was ok with it, so long as it was good clean fun and did not hurt anybody's self-respect. I do not think a game show that asks me to lose weight would hurt my pride at all, as long as I know where I stand.

8. Nowadays people seem to equate beauty with thinness; do you have any comments? Do you think that the society, media, etc., are reinforcing this idea?

I think this concept is typical of Asian thinking. If you do notice, artistes in the US or Europe, especially those very established and respected stars such as opera singers, they are not really that obsessed with this idea. However, we in Asia, are very much into this trend.

Personally, I feel it is difficult to define "thinness", as you can be stick-thin or slim yet has a curvaceous body. Therefore, being thin might not mean you are beautiful. I think to have a slender body with the right curves should be the correct way to view a body.

Also, I think this concept applies more to the ladies. I could be a fat guy walking on the street and people will only take a second look and that is all. But if it is a fat woman, people will start pointing their fingers and maybe gossip about her.

9. From your point of view, what makes a women pretty?

I feel that for a woman to look beautiful, she really needs to have some curves. God created man and woman to be different. So I am quite conservative on this matter and think that a woman should have a curvaceous body to look pretty. This criterion may not be a very good standard to go by, but I feel it is something a woman needs in order to look womanly. Or else, what is difference between a man and a woman, as nowadays the hairstyles are already quite the same! If the body shape looks the same between the sexes, then we might need to go to the toilet to tell them apart!

10. So having a curvaceous body does not necessarily mean having a thin body?

You can look good even though you are fat, but the shape has to be in proportion. It is quite normal to see a fat person's lower part of the body protruding, and it is not really nice. I am quite lucky that my lower body is not sticking out.

Talents Matter More Than Size
— Interview with Hossan Leong

Interviewed by
Editorial Team, World Scientific

S mall-framed actor-comedian Hossan Leong tells us how he gains confidence with his own body size, society's fixation on thinness and what makes a woman beautiful.

1. Does size matter to you? Have you tried in one way or another to reach your ideal size?

If you are talking about being a hunk, I would say that no, it doesn't matter to me anymore. But it used to bother me when I was much

younger. Especially in the entertainment business, where you either have to be a babe or a hunk to get anywhere in the business, which is not entirely fiction. It is quite true, you know. You see who gets to appear on the television nowadays? It is those who have a good looking face, have the body and the height.

So, I used to go to the gym to work out and try to build some muscles, but that was about three to four years ago. After a while, I felt that it was silly. Why am I trying to be somebody I am not?

Also, because of my erratic schedule for both television and stage, I am too tired to go to the gym nowadays. Once you are a stage actor, you do not have a life at all, you just work the whole day. So I keep fit in other ways, like playing games.

Gradually, I come to accept the fact that my body is slight, I am short and will never grow taller. But having said that, and I am not saying this because of sour grapes, I know for a fact that I have got more talent than anybody else on television. I don't need a body.

2. How long did it take for you come to this acceptance stage?

It was about five years ago when I was getting a bit deterred. It was then that I realised that I was struggling for roles that I know I will never get. So I thought, what's the point?

Then I told myself, instead of working on the outside, wouldn't it be better if I work on what's inside: my skills, my talents, and my personality. After a while, I slowly realise that I grow to be a much more gracious, much more giving and much more accepting person.

I realised that it is all about what I am, about what I can do for you. This is what it is all about at the end of the day, actually. It is not about how a person looks. But to a certain extent, as an actor, I have to look after my appearance of course.

3. Did anybody influence you on that, or is it yourself that make that change?

I think this is a learning process that one has to go through as a person, as you grow as an individual. It is not that anybody influences me or changes me, it is just a growing process that you have to come to terms with as an individual.

Some people unfortunately never grow out of it. Their self esteem remains low, they feel they will never be perfect, hence problems like anorexia, bulimia come into the picture, or they start to take steroids or go to the gym to make their bodies look big.

4. Being an actor, did you land with any plum roles because of your size, or has it caused some inconvenience instead?

At the end of the day, you see that, in Singapore anyway, there is noboby who can do what I do, or look what I look. I have conquered a niche market already. If you can find someone who look like me, and do what I do, then there will be some kind of "competition".

My niche in entertainment would be the fact that I am in theatre, that I can sing, dance and play the piano. I can also direct. I am in Chinese language and English language television programmes as well. And I can also speak French. Comedy is my forte, but I can do drama too.

There are so many different aspects to one's personality. I think it is wrong to say that you can be a star only if you look good. Why are you narrowing your prospects and opportunities for that matter?

5. So, at the end of the day, it is about what you are good at that matters most, right?

Yes. It's from inside out and not outside in. One of my good friends recently commented that I am now looking happier, more radiant. She thinks that I am also carrying myself better, as if I have been going to the gym. No, I said to her, I have stopped going to the gym. I only keep fit by playing tennis with my friends.

It is just that I am in a happy state, where you accept yourself as you are, rather than trying to be someone you might not be able to attain. So what if you have attained it, where is that benchmark? How far would you go, before you say this is the perfect state my body should be in? How do you know what is the prefect state? Where do you draw the line?

6. Now that you have achieved fame, do you then put in a conscious effort to stay like this?

Yes and no. There are not many things I do to maintain myself. The things I change are basically whether I shave or don't shave, whether I change my hair colour, whether I shorten my hair or not. Size wise, of course when we get older, we tend to get a loose tummy, which I need to take care of. So it means I have to play more tennis with my friends lah!

I do go to the gym once in a while, just to tone up and train a bit. Unfortunately, or fortunately, this is part of my actor's regime — training and discipline. You have to be physically fit, a demand that this job has on you. For an actor, the voice, the body, the outward appearance is important. If you go to an audition, and you look horrible, who's going to hire you?

7. There seems to be an obsession with thinness currently, any comments?

I would say I blame it all on media. I would blame it on the fact that concepts like "beautiful" equals "slim", "successful" equals "slim" perpetuated by the media has limited people's views. I also think it is a result of lack of education.

The subliminal message in advertisements is actually a kind of bombardment! In every page you turn, you see "slim" this, "slim" that.

So, if you are a heartlander, for example living in Seng Kang, and your concepts of success and beauty come from the television and magazines, you will say "oh, she's so beautiful, she is so thin, I want to be like her", when you see a glamorous and slim actress.

But I don't just blame the local media, it is media all around the world really. But the suffering that you have to go through to get the slim figure, it is just not worth it.

8. In local plays that you acted in, did they also reinforce this concept?

No. In theatre, we are more widely accepted as who we are, and we are hired for the fact that we can do our job, not for how we look. Of course, how we look would play a part. For example, if they were looking for someone to be Puck in "A Midsummer's Night Dream", they would not cast someone big and ungainly. But then again, who says you can't do that in theatre? It is just our perception.

It is about you that really gets you the job in theatre. One good example is the play, "Dim Sum Dolly", that I just did with Selena Tan, Pamela Oei and Emma Yong. We sold out! Why? Because people appreciate our talent! People know that they will have a good time at the play.

But unfortunately, television can't achieve that. Television can be switched on and off at free will, so what attract people to keep on watching are pretty faces and good bodies. It doesn't matter if you cannot act! People tune in to see pretty faces, while doing other things at the same time, such as cooking!

To the stations, this means ratings. To the advertisers, these are the things that will bring in the money for them.

9. From your point of view, what makes a women pretty? Does size play a part?

I think for me is what catches my eye. It does not have to be physical beauty; it can be a personality. I see a woman and what makes me look at her a second time does not need to be outward beauty. It can be the way she walks, the way she carries herself, that is attractive to look at.

Let me give you an example. When you are at a fashion show, you see one model, another model, and a third model walking on the runway. Then after a while, you think hey didn't I see her before? Why? Because they are all slim! And, if you go to the backstage of a fashion show and see a naked model, they look very ugly. They are just skin and bones. Is that your idea of beauty?

But, people have different ideas of what beauty should be. Personally for me, it has to radiate from somewhere, and definitely not from size of her waist.

10. If there is a plum role that requires you to gain a lot of weight within a stipulated time, would you consider taking it up?

It is not an issue. It is only a character that I play.

11. Aren't you afraid that you cannot go back to your original size?

No. I don't think it has been scientifically proven that once you get fat, you cannot slim down again. But if you do get fat and cannot slim down again, deal with it then, you accepted the role in the first place. I don't think it is going to be a problem.

12. If given the chance, would you like to trade places with Moses Lim?

I know Moses, I have worked with him before. He started off his career playing the fat-thin comedy duo with Jack Neo. I appreciate that, and there is nothing wrong with it. I have also worked with other people who are on the big side, they can dance and sing just as well. Size has nothing to do with their brilliance and their talents at all.

13. One last question, is there a fear of being stereotyped?

Of course, there is a fear of being stereotyped every time. But it is about how you pull yourself out of the situation.

Let's say the station calls and wants me to do another "Gurmit's World". It is up to me to say yes or no. If I do not want to be stereotyped or be cast in a supporting role ever again, I will say no. Why can't it be called Hossan's World?

It is about how you reinvent yourself. If I want to do comedy, then I will go ahead. If I want to do a musical, then I will do that. To people who says that I should only do comedy since I am a comedian, I will ask them, why I should pigeonhole myself?

The Trim and Fit (TAF) Programme
— The Route to Physical Fitness for School Children

Compiled by
Editorial Team, World Scientific

A ccording to a Singapore Ministry of Health report "The Health of Singaporeans 1993", obesity in students from primary, secondary and pre-university schools increased almost three-fold from 5.4% in 1980 to 15.1% in 1991.

In response to this trend, the Ministry of Education launched the Trim and Fit (TAF) Programme in 1992. The aim of the TAF programme is to improve physical fitness among schoolchildren in Singapore and reduce the percentage of overweight students.

With the anticipation that arresting the problem at an early stage could curb the rise of lifestyle diseases, the TAF programme is targeted at all students from the primary schools to pre-university levels. It emphasises a balance of physical activity with counselling in proper nutrition and diet to achieve a healthy lifestyle.

Under the TAF programme, schools are banded according to their Fitness Index. This index is derived from the average of the physical fitness test and overweight percentage results. Each year, schools in Band A will be given Gold awards. Silver awards will be given to those in Band B while schools in Band C and D will not receive any awards.

Table 1. Banding Criteria for TAF Awards 2001–2003

Bands		Secondary Schools
A (GOLD)	Fitness Index	79%
	Overweight %	8%
	Physical Fitness Test	72%
B (SILVER)	Fitness Index	70%
	Overweight %	11%
	Physical Fitness Test	57%
C	Fitness Index	61%
	Overweight %	13%
	Physical Fitness Test	40%
D	Fitness Index	Below Band C
	Overweight %	Above Band C
	Physical Fitness Test	Below Band C

Notes:

1. Fitness Index = (Acceptable Weight %* + % of Passes in Physical Fitness Test)

*Acceptable Weight % = 100% - % of Overweight Students - % of Underweight Students

2. To be placed in a particular band, a school must meet the criteria set for all three categories. For the fitness index and physical fitness pass rate, a school must attain or exceed the percentages set for the respective band. However, for the overweight percentage, the school must not exceed the percentage set for the respective band.

3. For example, to be placed in Band A, a secondary school must attain or exceed 79% and 72% set for the fitness index and physical fitness test pass rate respectively, but for the overweight percentage, it should not exceed 8%.

Source: www1.moe.edu.sg

For example, since 1992, Raffles Institution has been receiving the Silver awards under the TAF programme. Over the years, the school has made progressive improvement in performance in the annual National Physical Fitness Award (NAPFA) tests as well as in reducing the percentage of overweight pupils in the school. In 2001, the school was awarded the Trim and Fit Gold award for the third consecutive year.

To achieve positive results such as the above, schools are coming up with interesting programmes during their TAF sessions to help schoolchildren lose weight. At Raffles Girls School, TAF activities include endurance running, strength/weight training, games, interval training, martial arts and dance/low impact aerobics.

For primary schoolchildren, the activities would include less demanding exercise such as rope skipping. At Xinghua Primary School, daily TAF skipping sessions are carried out during the first ten minutes of every recess before the pupils proceed to the canteen for food.

Besides rope skipping, Xinghua pupils are exposed to both aerobic and anaerobic, such as endurance run, gymnastics, circuit training, stairs climbing, rope skipping and modified games. These TAF sessions are held twice a week and each session lasts 45 minutes.

And it has worked wonders! The percentage of overweight pupils in Xinghua went down by 3.64% from 13.06% in 1996 to 9.42% in 1997.

Overweight students are also required to follow strict dieting to complement their exercise routines. At Pioneer Junior College, all members of the TAF club are required to adopt a diet plan. They are to adhere to guidelines such as:

- No consumption of deep fried food, e.g., fast food and fried chicken wings;
- No consumption of sweet products that consist of higher portion of simple sugar, e.g., soft drinks, creamy cakes, creamy and sweet deserts, chocolates and sweets;
- No consumption of preserved or canned food, e.g., salted fish, salted egg and century egg, pickled fruits, dried salted fruit and fruit peel, hot dog and luncheon meat;
- No consumption of tidbits;
- Most importantly, increased intake of fresh vegetables and fruits;
- Reduce consumption of red meat, e.g., beef;
- Drink 8–10 glasses of water per day.

Parents of overweight students are also roped in to help their children fight the flab. They are encouraged to access the Ministry of Education's website at http://www.moe.gov.sg/

cpdd/pe/taf/ to download electronic brochures, where information is provided on how they can help their children stay trim and fit and maintain a healthy lifestyle.

Xinghua Primary invites parents of TAF students for a Meet-The-Parents session to create awareness among the parents so that they too can help the school's effort in shaping their children to lead a healthy lifestyle. At Pioneer, TAF club members and their parents are expected to attend a few diet-counselling sessions organised by the college.

Perhaps the most glowing report on the success rate of the TAF programme should fittingly come from the former Education Minister Teo Chee Hean himself. In his speech given at the 44th Annual General Meeting of the Singapore Schools Sports Councils delivered in early January 2003, he expressed delight towards the progress achieved by the programme over the years.

The percentage of the student population who passed the National Physical Fitness Test has improved from 57.8% in 1992 to 82.0% in 2002. The overall percentage of overweight students has reduced from 14.0% to 9.8%.

According to him, these steady improvements have come about as a result of more schools adopting a "whole-school" approach to the TAF programme. For these schools, the promotion of a healthy lifestyle among students is the joint responsibility of various stakeholders — school leaders, teachers, canteen vendors, students and parents.

Their commitment is seen in the innovative strategies that they have implemented to meet the needs of their students and engage them in healthy living habits. As a result, in 2003, a total of 291 schools received 124 Gold and 167 Silver awards in recognition of their efforts and achievements in the TAF scheme.

In addition, 14 junior colleges and two centralised institutes received the MINDEF Physical Fitness Performance Award (MPFPA) that year. These institutions have continued to make good progress in raising the physical fitness levels of their students.

The overall NAPFA Silver/Gold pass rate has increased from 75.6% in 2001 to 78.8% in 2002. In particular, the pass rate for female students has shown a significant improvement, from 76.8% in 2001 to 82.1% in 2002.

Sources:

http://www.moe.gov.sg/cpdd/pe/taf

http://www.sgnews.gov.sg/samplespeech/moe%20sample.htm

http://www.ri.sch.edu.sg/Departments/Pe/TAF_banding%20criteria%202003.htm

http://schools.moe.edu.sg/pjc/PJC_PE/TAF/trim_and_fit.htm

http://www.rgs.edu.sg/dept/pe/TAF.html

http://www.moe.edu.sg/schools/xinghua/TAF.htm

The Slimming Phenomenon
in Popular Culture

Joel Teo Woan Yee
Journalist
Lianhe Zaobao

"Thin equals beauty" is a popular concept that started to gain currency from the last century.

In recent years, it has graduated from outward appearance to the psychological level, as evidenced by the "thin is confidence" message espoused by the countless slimming advertisements.

To be slim is almost on everybody's mind, no thanks to the constant bombardment by advertisements and commercials. You will find that a girl who is neither fat nor thin will still harbour thoughts of dieting, because to maintain a slender figure has become the "in" thing to do in our present way of life.

The Slim 10 episode exposed two trends: one is the modern woman's desire to be slim and slender; the other is a malice of our present day society, that is, the reliance on drugs and special formula to get thin, instead of controlling food intake and regular exercise.

The female's obsession with "thinness" was born in the 1960s, when the matchstick-like models became international stars on the runway. In the 1980s, designers of the biggest fashion houses modelled their clothes after the thin and frail figures of runway supermodels. It was like saying, if you want to be stylish, be thin.

Not to be left out, pop musicians and movie stars who are on the thin side brought the message to an even wider audience of girls and women. Fans "love" their idols so much that they aspire to have the same body size.

At the same time, a "keep fit" trend has also started to creep into the modern lifestyle. From aerobics in the 1980s to attending gym and weight lifting sessions in recent years, now there is also yoga and vegetarianism. The emphasis on our body shape and weight has shifted from an aesthetics pursuit to becoming a way of life.

Of course, we do make a difference between people who practise yoga at the gym and people who go to slimming centres to get a thin figure. The former is working towards a long-term healthy lifestyle while the latter is searching for a quick fix on the bathing scale. While the objectives may differ, the results might actually have overlapping areas, such as achieving a fat-free body.

There is no age limit when it comes to wanting a slim figure, thanks to the constant bombardment of slimming advertisements. A mother who has given birth to a few kids can regain the body shape of her teenage years, best illustrated by those slender movie stars who are married with kids. To feel good and to hear praises about one's body always makes one happy. Those "aunties" who have the money and the time cannot help but to be "brainwashed" by these commercials.

But how do people really go about getting a thin figure? In the 1980s, women had to stick to an aerobics regime in order to slim down, but advances in technology and medicine has helped contemporary women switch to all kinds of slimming products. They can even have liposuctions. Newspapers blow up stories of how TV stars slimmed down successfully after taking certain kinds of dieting drugs. Cosmetic surgery has also become very commonplace nowadays. All these have encouraged people to take the easy way out. How many of us actually lose weight by exercising regularly and resisting high-calorie food? If you care to ask those who have maintained a slender figure for many years, you will not be surprised to hear that their secret is exercising and eating wisely. The doctor's advice to obese patients is also to cut down on food that are deep-fried and have high sugar content, and also to do exercise on a regular basis.

SLIM Chance FAT Hope

However, advanced technology and medical science have given us a chance to see quick results, hence people starts turning to slimming drugs. But after the Slim 10 saga, the barrage of slimming advertisements does not seem to have abated. People will still carry on consuming these products, although they have been warned of the consequences.

Reflections from the Movies

Eista Lee
Journalist
Lianhe Zaobao

I t is human instinct to seek beauty, and for the Chinese, the importance of this pursuit ranks as high as having a good meal.

There are many reasons why a person puts on too much weight; over-eating could be one of them. Some people turn to excessive shopping or eating when they are stressed up; the Hong Kong movie, "Love on a Diet" (starring Andy Lau and Sammi Cheng) is a good example.

Sammi Cheng played a character who went to Japan and fell in love with a handsome music student. After he left the country for further studies, she was so sad that she cried — and ate

— non-stop. When he returned to look for her, she was too fat and too ashamed to face him again. A lovelorn Sammi went to every concert she could, just to see him from afar. Then, she got to know a fat friend played by Andy Lau. After learning of her plight, he worked very hard to raise enough money so that she could go for dieting treatments at the hospital. A slim Sammi did not re-unite with the musician, instead she found herself pining for Andy. The two did live happily ever after, but it was only after Andy managed to shed off his extra pounds. The movie seems to tell us that man's biggest challenge is not to conquest the world but his own demons, and one of them is his body image.

In the Hollywood movie, "Shallow Hal", when the father of Jack Black's character was on his deathbed, he told his son to only date the youngest, prettiest women. Black did as he was told and only appreciated women for their surface. Then he was hypnotised into only seeing women for their inner beauty. So, when Black met the character played by Gwyneth Paltrow, he thought he has met the woman of his dreams. Others see Paltrow for what she was, a 300-pound woman, but Black could only see the beauty on the inside. When he woke up from the hypnotisation, he was horrified to see the real Paltrow.

The ending of this movie is untypical of Hollywood. Black followed his heart rather than his eyes and finally won over the big fat Paltrow. The message of this movie seems to be that if we love someone, we should not just look at his or her appearance but at the inner beauty and also accept the flaws.

In these two movies, the actresses wore fat suits to portray their overweight characters, whereas Taiwanese actress Yang

Huishan actually put on weight for her 1985 movie, "Kuei-Mei, A Woman". Audiences could still remember her slightly bulging tummy and a face as round as the moon. It was quite a feat during those years and was reported widely in the newspapers. Yang's superb performance and sacrifice for art's sake won her the Best Actress accolade at the Golden Horse Movie Awards.

Nearer to date, we saw Renée Zellweger piling on the pounds in real life for her character in the British comedy, "Bridget Jones's Diary". In it, Zellweger is a single thirty-something in a boring job and her only dreams are to lose weight and find true love. Hong Kong comedienne Sandra Ng also increased her weight by 5 kilograms to play the character of a prostitute in the movie, "Golden Chicken". She won rave reviews for her role and the movie enjoyed box office success.

Most of these movies that involve fat characters are comedies and the central roles usually need to overcome some sort of adversaries. "Love on a Diet" and "The Nutty Professor" starring Eddie Murphy went along this line and created box office successes. A recent Hong Kong film, "Running On Kharma", also saw Andy Lau donning a fat suit. But the storyline was slanted towards slapstick, as Andy had to do a striptease and participate in a bodybuilding competition in the movie. The only purpose was to show off his body, and there was no underlying message for the audience.

On the other hand, some "fat" roles are actually metaphors for the protagonists' twisted mentalities. The plump nurse in the 1996 movie "Deep Crimson", directed by Mexico's Arturo Ripstein, forced an invalid old man in a wheelchair to touch her bosom and make love to her. If the nurse had a slender figure, it might have lessened the impact that the movie had intended.

Body Image
A Big Deal*

Sharon Loh
Columnist
Sunday Times

T he business of thin is a fat one, and will be as long as there is demand for slimming products, and methods.

The appetite to be thin doesn't look like abating any time soon. Much as we like to cavil against the cancerous idea which has been perpetuated by the media, Hollywood, and business corporations that thin is perfection, it is a trend which has persisted for 40 years.

---

*This is an extract of the original article published in the *Sunday Times* on 27 July 2003.

The message, according to studies, has become culturally entrenched, pervading all age groups and socio-economic classes. Women are vulnerable whatever they weigh.

While a small number of women will go on to develop true eating disorders, there are many who will engage in risky behaviour just to achieve their ideal weight in the shortest time possible.

The relationship between a negative body image and risk taking behaviour is a complex one, taking into account many factors, such as an individual's mental state, stage of life, personal history, and the characteristics of the society she lives in.

There are two choices in tackling this: either we roll over as victims, or we try and fight this fallacy, both as individuals and a community.

As a community we in Singapore have not done enough to debunk the ridiculous notion that women should aspire to be underweight.

It may be like swimming against the tide to take such a pervasive idea head on, but capitulating could mean far worse, as the tragic stories of the Slim 10 victims tell.

The Victoria state government in Australia is trying at least. It is working on gender portrayal guidelines that it will promote to the advertising industry to try and improve the way women are depicted in advertising.

Singapore, with its love of campaigns, should consider a programme to promote a healthy body image among our young. Schools could include self-esteem courses; community health groups could conduct workshops on how to be healthy at one's weight, rather than thin at any cost.

Many will say, there's nothing wrong with wanting to be thin. I say, there's something wrong with never liking yourself over 45kg.

As someone constantly looking for the perfect diet, I received a rude wake up call one day when my four-year-old daughter stood in front of the mirror in an empire-cut dress and moaned, "But it makes me look fat."

I realised that I had to take the blame for what was happening in her head.

Body image attitudes are developed in childhood. The strong messages of body shape, sexual attractiveness and beauty learnt by children are learnt well before puberty. It's with them that we can break the downward spiral.

If it's about who's responsible, then we all are.

To Fight an Ever Losing Battle
— A Personal Account

Lam Wai Kit
Journalist
Lianhe Zaobao

R ecently I attended quite a few weddings and ran into old friends whom I had not seen for a long time. Invariably, the first thing they said to me would always be, "It's been a long time, but you do not seem to have changed a bit. You are still as tall and big. I can recognise you from afar."

The truth is, I have changed a lot, at least the waistline has expanded quite a bit. If I could sell my pounds of flesh to restaurants for their dish making, I would have made a pile.

I too had my "slender" days, but it was in the good old days before I went to primary school. After that, my body shape changed drastically.

I remember I was sick and had to be hospitalised for a few days. My body size was normal during the hospital stay, but after I was discharged, it inflated like a balloon.

Sometimes, when I am chatting with friends, they would tease me, "The doctors must have given you a 'special jab' that makes you so fat and chubby!" I am actually quite amused when I heard that.

To many who have a large body size, the words "fat" or "chubby" are taboo and cannot be uttered in front of them, or else they will blow their top.

I am the exact opposite, I do not mind at all. When friends joke about my body size, I even laugh with them. These harmless banters would not make me lose any sweat. If they can really make me perspire and help me to slim down, I wish my friends could joke about me more!

It is because I know I am really on the big side. Rather than getting angry about it, it would be good if I can provide some laughter to my friends. Then at least there would be some value in my fatness.

Why do I become so fat? I have not done any research, though I believe that it has got to do with my diet when I was a kid.

I was the only grandson in my family and my grandmother doted on me. She bought me any food that I wanted to eat. Before I realised it, my appetite had increased substantially and there was no turning back.

Because of this reason, I am very tempted to tell some parents off whenever I see them let their children eat and drink without any restraint. I wish to tell them that if they do not control their children's food intake, the kids will grow up to be like me and it will be too late to regret.

So, when I have my own children in the future, I will not let them eat indiscriminately. Experience has taught me that loving them does not mean spoiling them. If they grow up to be obese, they are the ones who have to suffer the consequences, not us the parents, no matter how much we love them. The children also have to diet and slim down on their own efforts.

My first real effort to lose weight was in Secondary Three. Before that it was always talk and no action. But when I reached Secondary Three, the Ministry of Education made it compulsory for all overweight students to shed off their extra pounds.

We obese students were gathered to form a FAT (Fit and Trim) Club. The following year, the name was changed to TAF (Trim and Fit) Club, which rhymed with "tough", thereby instilling a sense of encouragement.

The person in-charged of the programme in my school was a young Physical Education teacher. We "went through hell" under his punishing regime of exercises. I could guarantee that all the club members would still remember him after all these years!

Every afternoon after school we were required to go for an exercise session, be it badminton in the school hall, lifting weight in the gym or running around the reservoir.

The reservoir was just directly across our school, so it became a convenient place for us to exercise. One round of the reservoir was equivalent to 6.6 km, and it seemed like a never-ending road to us!

SLIM Chance FAT Hope

Whenever the legs began to tire, we would slow down our pace, thinking nobody would spot us in the woods. But our instructor from hell was already equipped with a pair of binoculars on the other side of the water spying on us. The moment anybody slacked off, he would bellow from his loudspeaker to warn us to keep up our pace. We would jump from his shouting and started to run again.

He would not even let us off during recess times and recruited the help of the home economics teachers to restrict us from eating this or drinking that.

I put in so much effort, but my body shape did not change much. All my efforts had gone down the drain, and I really did not know what went wrong.

In junior college, I exercised much less, but my weight managed to stay within a "reasonable" range. Conveniently, "to lose weight" became the last thing on my mind. Throughout my National Service and university days, I was the same chubby self.

When I started to work, a busy schedule gave me the perfect excuse to relax and do nothing during the weekends. For a lazy person like me, the best thing that could happen was to pop some pills to slim down. Safety never really crossed my mind, as I was quite determined on this matter: to slim down in the shortest time possible.

I tried all kinds of slimming products, from fat burners to pills that stop the body from taking in sugar or speed up the metabolic rate and many more. Initially, some of them were as effective as the advertisements touted them to be. But, as I found out, the dosage needed to be increased in order for the effect to stay. I gave up after realising this. I would rather not become a perennial pill-popper.

Advertisements have a way of convincing fat people like us to believe in them. One such advertisement said that we only need a certain amount of money for a slimming treatment, which seems to me a fair price to pay. But when I turned up at the centre, I found out that the amount stated in the advert was limited to one session and on one part of the body only. If you want them to work on other areas, you have to pay extra!

There is another shocking discovery, that those who are successful in slimming down actually go to the slimming centre everyday! How on earth could I afford such an expense?

To think of it, fat people seem quite gullible. Whenever we hear of a new way to lose weight, it would seem like a godsend to us.

Before

After

Some of the methods are not really reliable, though. Such as wounding a finger with bandage, to eat chilli or apples in big amount... are they really effective?

Luckily, I am quite tall. Standing at 1.9 metre, my body shape is fortunately not rotund. Some of my friends actually told me that I do not need to lose weight, as I have the height to carry the weight.

Well, if they could try carrying my weight, they would not have said those words.

My weight tends to limit my movement, and it has contributed to a more sedentary lifestyle. It is actually quite difficult for me to get up and exercise. So, you guessed it, the result would be a vicious cycle, I put on more weight!

So, it seems like I need to put in more determination and will-power to lose weight. If you know where I can buy these two things, please tell me!

Towards a Healthy
Lifestyle

Exercise
Your Way to
Health and Fitness

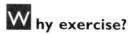

W hy exercise?

Different people get into regular exercise for different reasons. You do it to improve your appearance, as a form of family interaction, or just to keep yourself healthy.

The World Health Organisation states that sedentary lifestyles increase all causes of mortality, double the risk of cardiovascular diseases, diabetes and obesity; and increase the risk of colon cancer, high blood pressure, osteoporosis, lipid disorder, depression and anxiety.

Whether you are 16 or 60, regular exercise with sensible nutrition will help make a happier and healthier you.

How often?

You should be engaging in moderate physical activity for up to 30 minutes everyday. As long as you can maintain the level of intensity of your activity and still have a conservation with some effort, you are in the moderate zone. It is important to consult your physician prior to engaging in any exercise programme.

Ready, get set, go!

Dress light, feel right!

Avoid wearing loose-fitting clothing and remove all jewellery. Such items pose a definite danger, as they may get caught in the moving parts of the machines.

Stretch, warm-up, stretch!

Before you get into your warm-up, take a minute or two to do some very light stretches. This is especially important for those who are returning to regular exercise after a long sedentary lifestyle. Doing very light stretches first helps to prepare your unaccustomed body for the warm-up. Get into your real stretching after you have properly warmed up for at least 5–10 minutes.

Motivation

Variety

You need to vary your workouts in order to prevent burnout. Keep yourself informed of new, more challenging moves and techniques. Enhance your treadmill cardio workout with some strength training using resistance bands or free weights. Or invest in an elliptical cross-trainer, and alternate your runs with a proven zero-impact, calorie-burner.

Goal-oriented

Setting and monitoring goals is crucial to the success of your fitness programme. Be realistic too. If exercise is a priority in your busy schedule, then you may have to sacrifice a less important event. Make use of technological aids to help chart your progress. Many cardio-machines like treadmills and cross-trainers, have variable resistance that you can first benchmark, and then gradually increase as your fitness level improves.

Rewards

You deserve a reward when you reach your goal. The rewards do not have to be tangible. It could be as simple as taking pride in how your old clothes fall better on your new body, or just noticing your extra energy when you play with your kids.

Buddy

Find an exercise buddy to give you that little push to help you reach your goals. Arrange to work together for short periods at a time, like 2-3 months. If you have only one stationary bike, you two can still work out together. One could cycle while the other skips rope, and then rotate between the two exercises. Then you could take turns supporting each other during the strength-conditioning exercises.

Support

Support can come from many sources. Enlist the help of friends, colleagues and family, and get them to help you choose healthier foods. Schedule after-work drinks after your workout. Plan family activities around your workouts.

Workout and eat right

Determine your Target heart rate (THR)

Ever wonder if you are exercising at the right intensity level? Your Target Heart Rate (THR) is a simple yet effective way to help you determine your intensity level. This is expressed as a percentage of your Maximum Heart Rate (MHR). MHR is the theoretical maximum number of beats per minute that an average heart can pump. To find your approximate MHR, just follow the formula: 220 – (your age).

For example, you are 30 years old, then your MHR should be about 190. If you are just starting to get into regular exercise, you may want to take things slower. Try working out at 50% of your MHR, which would be 95.

What is your THR zone?

Next, take a look at the chart below. It is divided into three separate zones. To help you achieve your goals, each zone represents a distinct level of exertion. Your THR zone gives you the flexibility to work at your desired level of exertion, without worrying about keeping to a fixed number of heartbeats per minute.

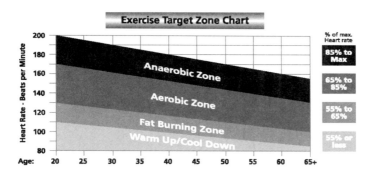

Tips to eating right

Moderation, not deprivation. Many of us cannot bear the thought of giving up our favourite foods, especially on doctor's orders. If we maintain regular exercise and practise moderate diet, there is a good chance that we can still enjoy our favourite foods!

Simple and sensible. Try to eat simply more often: vegetables, steamed rice, and a little fish or meat. Have a ready supply of fresh fruits that you can snack on, especially if you tend to feel peckish between meals.

Take small steps. Make small changes gradually, and give yourself time to adapt and accept. Each modification you make must become a habit, a new eating or lifestyle habit. This will ensure the changes become a permanent part of your life.

Designing a home gym

If you decide that working out at home is the most practical approach, the first consideration will be the location of the equipment. You may select an inspiring environment and inviting location that is well ventilated and provides sufficient lighting.

Benefits of using fitness equipment

Treadmills

Joggers that run outdoor on hard surface frequently may suffer from knee and ankle injuries. Therefore, it is safer to run on a treadmill with shock-absorption or cushioned deck to reduce jarring effect.

There are two types of treadmills: magnetic and motorised. Magnetic treadmills require kinetic energy to work and motorised treadmills require electricity supply to operate.

Treadmills are the most efficient equipment to burn calories and lose weight and can fit into any walkers or runners' busy schedule. Interval training programmes provided on most motorized treadmills offers you a variety of benefits. Firstly, it brings on a new challenge, breaking away from monotony from your current programmes. Secondly, it activates the body, thereby breaking through plateaus that you may be experiencing. Thirdly, due to the variance in the programme, the body is consistently overloading the heart and lungs, increasing endurance level and improving cardiovascular training!

Elliptical cross-trainer

Elliptical cross-trainers offer a no-impact workout that exercises numerous muscle groups. This is achieved through the dual cross-trainer arms combined with the foot pedals. They provide the following advantages:

- Time Efficiency: The dual action of arms and legs optimises energy expenditure; requires less time to achieve more results.
- Weight Bearing Exercise: Builds bone density and burns calories more efficiently. Inhibits the onset of osteoporosis.
- No Impact, Safe for Joints: Ideal workout for people with back, knee, hips and joint problems.
- Low Maintenance: Less impact means less wear and tear.
- Small Footprint: Does not take up valuable floor space.

Exercise bikes

Cycling is a very effective workout for those who suffer from knee problems or arthritis. Those who exercise regularly on an exercise bike will see great improvement in their health overtime.

Exercise bikes are great for cardiovascular fitness and toning/building your thighs. The exercise bike is also a great leg builder. You will develop and strengthen the quadriceps muscles, the gluteus muscles, and the hamstring muscles. There is virtually no impact from your upper weight so it is easy on your knees and joints and provides a good cardiovascular workout.

There are basically two types of exercise bikes you can use, upright bikes and recumbent bikes. The recumbent bike offers more back support and may be a little more comfortable to those people with lower back pain. For overweight exercisers, this bike offers bucket seats that are more comfortable than traditional uprights. It is also more ergonomically correct than a traditional upright bike, as well as an effective way to improve aerobic capacity and burn fat. Recumbent bikes also stress the gluteus muscles more so than with traditional upright bikes. For those who want to develop the butt, a recumbent exercise bike may be of interest.

Multi-gym station

The mental and physical stresses of daily life take a toll in the form of backaches, sore joints and headaches. Proper strength training can do a great deal to eliminate those aches and pains.

Studies have shown that strength training employed properly by people in their 60s or even 80s, can not only improve longevity but also improve their quality of life. As we age, our bones and joints weaken. Strength training not only helps support the bones and joints and lessen the impact of their weakening, but also improves coordination, muscle control and mobility.

One pound of fat weighs the same as one pound of muscle, but one pound of fat takes up five times the volume or space as one pound of muscle. Muscle, even at rest, burns calories (typically ten calories per pound of muscle per day) while fat burns no calories. If you increase your muscle mass you can use up more calories (even while you are asleep), and if you replace fat with muscle you can reduce your waistline at the same time.

Heart Rate Monitor

Benefits of using the Heart Rate Monitor:
- Maximise your exercise time and accelerate your performance
- Lose weight and tone up by burning fat instead of muscle

- Improve health and fitness by strengthening your heart and lungs
- Exercise more effectively by preventing over and under training
- Achieve your competitive edge by increasing endurance and preventing injury
- Target Heart Zone Rate Training
  - o Effective conditioning requires that you maintain your heart rate at the proper level of at least 20 minutes per workout. At too high a heart rate, your activity can be counter effective.
  - o The Fat Burning Zone, 55-65%, is recommended for those who have not worked out for a long time, trying to lose weight, high risk for heart problems or just not feeling 100% that day.
  - o The Aerobic Zone, 65-85%, is recommended for those in good physical condition, and have been exercising on a consistent basis for an extended period of time. Exercising at this range helps improve your fitness level and prevent injury caused from over training.
  - o The Anaerobic Zone, 85%-MHR, is to be used by ultra-athletes only and never recommended without close medical approval or supervision. This range is used only for those in extremely good physical condition during races or training for competition.

AIBI Healthtronics

If you are not game for action and prefer to take an effortless approach towards looking great, AIBI Healthtronics is the perfect device in helping you to slim down and tone up effectively.

AIBI Pro 12

The Pro 12 is a professional 12 pads and 12 programmes system. The 12 pads allow you to stimulate exercise in any three areas (abs, thighs and arms or busts) at one time. Experience professional quality in the comfort of your home or office offered by AIBI Pro 12 for toning and body building, pain and stress relieving, cellulite reducing and bust uplifting.

AIBI Compact 4

For those on the go, a portable 4 pads and 3 programmes system called Compact 4 can be operated by either an adaptor or a 9 volt battery. Select Body Toning, Shiatsu Massage or Relaxation mode as desired.

AIBI Facial Toner

Benefits of using AIBI Facial Toner:
- Tone up facial muscles, equivalent to a "face lift" without the surgery
- Reduce fine lines around eyes and mouth
- Firm up sagging skin and muscles

- Tighten a double chin
- Improve puffy eyes and dark circles under the eyes

It can be used on the mouth and cheeks, chin and jaw line, eyes and upper cheek, and neck. It is advisable to remove make-up from areas to be toned prior to using Facial Toner.

You may either apply the Facial Toner Gel with Collagen on the contact points of the Facial Toner equipment or simply moisten skin with the Facial Toner Gel with Collagen. With the contact points touching your skin, switch on the units and increase the output until you feel the sensation of muscle contractions. Increase the output as per your desire.

The Facial Toner Set includes a pair of Facial Toner equipment, a Facial Toner Gel with Collagen, a 9 volt battery, a copy of instruction booklet and a casing for portability. Additional accessories as attachments include single cable Facial Toner, bust cups, adhesive pads and cable.

Body Wrap Treatment

The Body Wrap Package includes Body Wrap Gel, Seaweed Wrap Gel, Mud Wrap, thermal film and a measurement tape.

Body Wrap Gel: An aromatherapy concoction of Aloe Vera, Zedoary Oil, Cinnamon Oil, Ginger Oil and Tea Tree Oil.

Seaweed Wrap Gel: The luxurious blend of Seaweed extracts, Rosemary, Fennel and Tea Tree Oil help to stimulate the lymphatic system. The presence of seaweed particles acts as an exfoliating agent, leaving the skin smoother, softer and enhanced the effects of body wrapping with Body Wrap Gel.

Mud Wrap: Body Wrapping with Mud Wrap, deep cleanse and condition your skin. Feel clean and refreshed even after the first session.

You just need to remember a simple 3-step procedure: Warm up, Massage and Wrap. You may warm up the gels by placing the gel tub in warm water. It is important to note that the gels need to be warm to touch. Do not heat gels in a microwave or in boiling water. Mud wrap can be used at room temperature. Apply the gel to the targeted areas of your body using firm, circular movements to encourage lymphatic drainage. Apply thermal film with a reasonable amount of pulling pressure as you wrap. Allow the width of the film to overlap by 1.5–2 inches with each turn. Always apply film starting with the furthest point, for example, begin with your calves if you are wrapping your leg or wrists if you are wrapping your arms.

Lose two inches and more after each treatment. Inch loss varies from person to person. The effects are likely to last up to 24 hours.

A simple home gym programme

The most important step is to actualise your fitness regime for a healthier and livelier you! We have come up with the following packages to suit your different needs and assist you to achieve a sculptured body and balanced mind.

For each of the following packages, select one item each from A and B:

Beginner Package (Trim)
A) AIBI Healthtronic Compact 4 / RS-248 Magnetic Treadmill / TE-326 Two-Way Air Bike

B) 3-in-1 Body Wrap / Acumen Basix Plus / Plus ES / B200 Sit-up Bench

Intermediate Package (Tone)

A) E-6700 Elliptical Cross-Trainer / HS-4950HR Magnetic Bike
B) AIBI Healthtronic Compact 4 / B-1001 multi-function Weight Bench

Advanced Package (Fit)

A) LT-1200 Motorised Treadmill / ST-950 Elliptical Cross-Trainer
B) AIBI Healthtronics Pro 12 / GY-9012 Multi-Gym Station

Professional Package (Anaerobic)

A) T3i Life Fitness Treadmill / X3i Life Fitness Cross-Trainer
B) EXM-1500 Multi-Gym Station / AB-B680R Recumbent Bike

Purchases can be made at all AIBI showrooms in Singapore. Please call 6533 8555 for enquiries. Kindly present this page to enjoy the above packages at special rates, subject to availability of the products at the point of purchase.

Source: Information in this chapter is provided by courtesy of AIBI International Pte Ltd.

Slimming Versus Losing Weight
— A TCM View from Eu Yan Sang

Introduction

Eu Yan Sang was founded in 1879 and has become a household name in Asia over the last 120 years. The company's mission is to care for mankind by helping consumers realise good life-long health. This rests on a relentless pursuit for quality products which are scientifically proven. In doing so, it stays abreast of advances in Traditional Chinese Medicine (TCM), and carves a niche in the provision of comprehensive healthcare services, without losing sight of the "Eu Yan Sang" spirit.

The company, with its headquarters in Singapore, continuously ensures that quality is maintained in the manufacturing of Chinese medicinal products and provision of modern Chinese medical services — a testimony to the healthy image and noble philosophy Eu Yan Sang upholds. More than 150 products are now manufactured and sold under the "Eu Yan Sang" brand, including proprietary medicine, healthcare products and tonics.

Interview with Eu Yan Sang's Clinical Physician

In a bid to offer readers the opportunity to better understand obesity from the Traditional Chinese Medicine's (TCM) point of view, the editorial team interviewed Eu Yan Sang's Senior Chinese Medicine Consultant Cao Bei. Dr. Cao doubles up as a TCM specialist at Eu Yan Sang's YourHealth TCM Centre. She graduated from Beijing's Chinese Medicine College in 1985 and is currently pursuing a Master of Science degree in Exercise and Nutrition with a university in Britain. Dr. Cao hopes to also view obesity from a modern scientific perspective and in turn integrate the best of Chinese and Western treatments. The following are extracts of the interview.

Chinese have been known to be food connoisseurs and used to perceive fatness (often thought to be synonymous with prosperity) to be beautiful. Today, the perception has changed and people scorn even the mention of the word "fat". So, what is TCM's perception of obesity?

We have been using body mass index (BMI) to define obesity: a BMI of more than 30 equals obesity, while about 25 is overweight. However, this definition has been revised by the World Health Organisation since the year 2003 to take into account Asians' smaller built. The revised definition points overweight to be between 22 and 23 and obesity as between 25 and 26. TCM does not quantify obesity, it divides obesity into two types — sthenia syndrome *(shi zheng)* or asthenia syndrome *(xu zheng)*.

A sufferer of the former is full of energy, has bad breath and his stool is hard while one who suffers from asthenia syndrome feels weak, is prone to flu and his stool is soft. Generally speaking, most of the obese suffer from the asthenia syndrome. Many who suffer from sthenia syndrome turn asthenia with time. TCM believes that one suffers from the asthenia syndrome because of deficiency in the vital energy *(qi)* and the state of blood. It is also probable that the person has not extracted sufficient nutrients from the food he consumes. Many thought obesity is a result of over-nutrition, but malnutrition warrants more attention.

TCM attributes obesity to the following reasons: hindered circulation of body fluids or reduced metabolism — the body absorbs a lot but retains much of the toxic, thus blocking the meridian — and obstructed blood circulation which also blocks the meridian.

Chinese medicine believes there is a distribution network for the fundamental substances of *qi*, blood and body fluids throughout the body. The distribution network is known as the Meridian System and it transports *qi*, blood and body fluids. The system explains how one becomes sick.

Three components, on the other hand, make up calories: basic metabolism, calories extracted from food we consume and activities and exercises. In other words, when one is ill, one's basic metabolism slows down and the detoxification capability is reduced. The comprehensive way to control weight and stay healthy is therefore maintaining a moderate amount of calories, extracting sufficient nutrients and exercising regularly to attain a healthy basic metabolic rate.

So, what does slimming entail?

A Japanese professor once pointed out that those who really need to slim down turn a deaf ear to it or is not keen, and most of those keen to slim down are not "fat" per se. This explains why the genuine objective in slimming is to cut down on cholesterol. This will in turn, prevent illnesses caused by obesity.

Slimming differs from losing weight. Slimming mainly involves cutting down on fats. Shedding weight may just mean reducing water (instead of "oil") retained in the body .

There are many misconceptions about slimming, including aborting a slimming method should it fail to achieve the intended result in a month or two and adopting another, as well as little understanding about slimming products sold over the counter. Some who are not fat jump on the slimming bandwagon in pursuit of a slim body. Their ways of controlling appetitite without knowledge of the cause of obesity or their body constitution may ultimately be detrimental to their health.

How does TCM treat the obese?

This can be divided into internal and external treatments. The former means using medicine to control one's appetite so as to achieve the bodily balance. This is to prevent the body from absorbing too much toxic and to speed up metabolic rate. External treatment, on the other hand, includes acupuncture, rubbing, scraping the patient's neck, chest or back, cupping and auriculotheraphy or ear-acupuncture. The external treatment has

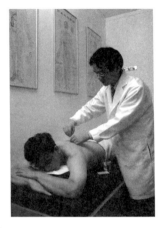

to go hand in hand with the internal ones to achieve the desired slimming outcome.

TCM uses a customerised or individualised approach; acupuncture is not suitable for everyone, for instance. A physician has to exercise his discretion and understand a person's body constitution to help to treat the person scientifically.

According to a survey in China, those aged between 20 and 50 years are more suitable for acupuncture. This is because the bodily development has not been stabilised before one turns 20, while for those over 50 years old, the bodies have been shaped and it is difficult to speed up their metabolism rates. The duration of a course of acupuncture treatment for the purpose of slimming also differs for different people.

TCM adjusts the meridian system to improve metabolism or aid in the resolution of body cholesterol, so that a person is healthy again. In helping a person to slim down, TCM persistently controls his appetite or regulates excess absorption and digestive functions. However, one who wants to undergo TCM treatment would still have to top it up with healthy food consumption and regular exercises.

What types of Chinese medicine aid in slimming?

Again, a person has to watch his body constitution when buying Chinese medicine. There are in fact more than 50 types of Chinese medicine which can directly aid in slimming. Each of them fulfils a special purpose. For instance, Hawthorn Berry (cratagegus pinnatifida or *shanzha*), sickle senna (cassia tora or *jue ming zi*), lotus leaves and Polygonum Knotweed root (*he shou wu*) are thought to aid in reducing blood cholesterol and weight.

jue ming zi

shanzha

he shou wu

In slimming, can we integrate both Chinese and Western treatments?

Yes, although many in Singapore seem sceptical and are worried that the two types of medicine "clash" with each other, China has been integrating the two to nurse health. The topic is also a much debated one in the Mainland. Regardless of which medicine is used, it is to nip the problem in the bud. One has to have a good knowledge of both medicines and know their functions to make them complement each other in treating obesity.

With so many products for slimming and dieting available on the market, how should consumers choose to ensure the safety and effects of such products?

According to a survey in China, consumers hold effects and safety as their top priorities. In other words, slimming should not have side effects, one should not revert to one's original weight easily and the price of the treatment should not be too steep. I wish to reiterate that consumers who wish to slim down should understand their body constitution and consult physicians.

Are there ways to slim down instantaneously?

The ideal slimming result is not more than five kilograms in a month, or not more than 1.5 kilograms a week. Our weight increases slowly with time, the same should apply to slimming. We cannot ask for quick results but have to watch our diet and exercise more.

In exercising, one has to pay attention to the following:

- How regular: to slim down, one has to exercise three to four days a week, the duration each day should be at least 40 minutes. If it is fewer than 30 minutes, one is only burning away carbohydrates. The results achieved by an exercise session that lasts 40 minutes are similar to an accumulated exercise regime of 40 minutes in a day.
- How vigorous: moderate exercises are best for burning fats, thus, brisk walk or slow jog is sufficient; do not undergo very intensive exercises.
- To slim down, exercise on an empty stomach. However, one should not be starving when one exercises.
- It is noted that air quality in the evenings is best and thus suitable for outdoor exercises.

Index